CUPCAKES

Bounty Books and ACP Magazines Ltd hereby
exclude all liability to the extent permitted by law for
any errors or omissions in this book and for any loss,
damage or expense (whether direct or indirect) suffered
by a third party relying on any information contained
in this book.

First published in 2006 by ACP Magazines Ltd

This edition published in 2011 by Bounty Books,
a division of Octopus Publishing Group Ltd,
Endeavour House, 189 Shaftesbury Avenue, London WC2H 8JY
www.octopusbooks.co.uk

An Hachette UK Company
www.hachette.co.uk

ISBN: 978-0-753722-31-2

Printed and bound in China

THE AUSTRALIAN
Women's Weekly

CUPCAKES

Bounty
Books

contents

introduction

These exquisite little cakes are ideal for afternoon tea, as an elegant and chic dessert for a dinner party, or as a splendid and original birthday cake. While it's true they look like little works of art, and a few of them require some cake decorating experience, most of them are not difficult to make. We have had the best fun dreaming up ideas for the design of these little masterpieces, and playing with the flavours so they complement the look of the cakes.

veryberry cakes

Dried berry buttercake

125g butter, softened
½ teaspoon vanilla extract
⅔ cup (150g) caster sugar
2 eggs
1 cup (150g) dried mixed berries
½ cup (70g) slivered almonds
⅔ cup (100g) plain flour
⅓ cup (50g) self-raising flour
¼ cup (60ml) milk

Sugared fruit

150g fresh blueberries
120g fresh raspberries
1 egg white, beaten lightly
2 tablespoons vanilla sugar

Cream cheese frosting

30g butter, softened
80g cream cheese, softened
1½ cups (240g) icing sugar

1 Prepare sugared fruit.
2 Preheat oven to moderately low (170°C/150°C fan-assisted). Line 6-hole large or 12-hole standard muffin tray with paper cases.
3 Beat butter, vanilla extract, sugar and eggs in small bowl with electric mixer until light and fluffy.
4 Stir in fruit and nuts, then sifted flours and milk. Divide mixture among cases; smooth surface.
5 Bake large cakes about 45 minutes, small cakes about 35 minutes. Turn cakes onto wire rack to cool.
6 Make cream cheese frosting.
7 Spread cakes with frosting. Decorate with sugared fruit.

Sugared fruit

Brush each berry lightly with egg white; roll fruit in sugar. Place fruit on baking parchment-lined tray. Leave about 1 hour or until sugar is dry.

Cream cheese frosting

Beat butter and cheese in small bowl with electric mixer until light and fluffy; gradually beat in sifted icing sugar.

pear butterfly cakes

Pear and maple buttercake

1 medium fresh pear (230g),
  grated coarsely
60g butter, softened
¼ cup (35g) self-raising flour
¾ cup (110g) plain flour
1 teaspoon ground cinnamon
½ cup (110g) firmly packed
  brown sugar
¼ cup (60ml) maple-flavoured
  syrup
2 eggs
⅓ cup (40g) coarsely chopped
  pecans
⅓ cup (55g) finely chopped
  dried pear

Pear butterflies

1 tablespoon caster sugar
1 tablespoon water
1 medium brown pear (230g)
  (eg. beurre bosc), sliced thinly

Fondant icing

500g white prepared fondant
  icing, chopped coarsely
1 egg white
blue, pink and yellow food
  colouring

1 Make pear butterflies.
2 Preheat oven to moderate
(180°C/160°C fan-assisted). Line
6-hole large or 12-hole standard
muffin tray with paper cases.
3 Drain fresh pear, squeezing out
as much juice as possible. You
need ⅔ cup grated pear.
4 Beat butter, flours, cinnamon,
sugar, syrup and eggs in small
bowl with electric mixer on low
speed until ingredients are
combined. Beat on medium
speed until mixture is changed
to a paler colour.
5 Stir in fresh pear, nuts and
dried pear. Divide mixture
among cases; smooth surface.
6 Bake large cakes about
35 minutes, small cakes about
30 minutes. Turn cakes onto
wire rack to cool.
7 Make fondant icing. Divide
icing into three small bowls;
using colourings, tint icing pale
blue, pink and yellow. Spoon
icing quickly over cakes, level
with tops of cases; allow to set.
8 Top cakes with pear slices.

Pear butterflies

Preheat oven to very low (120°C/
100°C fan-assisted). Combine
sugar and the water in small
saucepan. Stir over medium
heat, without boiling, until sugar
is dissolved. Bring to a boil,
reduce heat; simmer, without
stirring, 1 minute. Brush pear
slices both sides with sugar
syrup. Place slices in a single
layer on a wire rack over oven
tray (see page 125). Dry in
oven about 40 minutes. While
pears are still warm, shape into
butterfly wings (see page 125).
Cool on wire rack.

Fondant icing

Place fondant in a medium
bowl over a medium saucepan
of simmering water; stir until
smooth. Stir in egg white.
Stand at room temperature
for about 10 minutes or until
thickened slightly.

Chocolate ginger cake

½ cup (110g) firmly packed
   brown sugar
½ cup (75g) plain flour
½ cup (75g) self-raising flour
¼ teaspoon bicarbonate of soda
1 teaspoon ground ginger
½ teaspoon ground cinnamon
¼ teaspoon ground nutmeg
90g butter, softened
1 egg
¼ cup (60ml) buttermilk
2 tablespoons golden syrup
50g dark eating chocolate,
   chopped coarsely

Decorations

300ml whipping cream
3 x 50g chocolate-covered
   honeycomb bars, chopped
   coarsely

1 Preheat oven to moderately low (170°C/150°C fan-assisted). Line 6-hole large or 12-hole standard muffin tray with paper cases.
2 Sift dry ingredients into small bowl, add butter, egg, buttermilk and syrup; beat mixture with electric mixer on low speed until ingredients are combined. Increase speed to medium, beat until mixture is changed to a paler colour. Stir in chocolate. Divide mixture among cases; smooth surface.
3 Bake large cakes about 40 minutes, small cakes about 30 minutes. Turn cakes onto wire rack to cool.
4 Spread cakes with whipped cream; top with chopped honeycomb.

honeycomb creams

Vanilla buttercake

90g butter, softened
½ teaspoon vanilla extract
½ cup (110g) caster sugar
2 eggs
1 cup (150g) self-raising flour
2 tablespoons milk

Butter cream frosting

125g butter, softened
1½ cups (240g) icing sugar
2 tablespoons milk
50g dark eating chocolate,
   chopped finely
1 tablespoon cocoa powder
pink food colouring

Decorations

ice cream waffle cones
strawberry slices
toasted coconut flakes
finely grated dark eating
   chocolate

1 Preheat oven to moderate (180°C/160°C fan-assisted). Line 6-hole large or 12-hole standard muffin tray with paper cases.
2 Beat butter, extract, sugar, eggs, flour and milk in small bowl with electric mixer on low speed until ingredients are just combined. Increase speed to medium, beat until mixture is changed to a paler colour.
3 Divide mixture among cases; smooth surface.
4 Bake large cakes about 25 minutes, small cakes about 20 minutes. Turn cakes onto wire rack to cool.
5 Make butter cream frosting.
6 Remove cases from cakes. Using a serrated knife, shape cakes into balls (see page 124) so they sit inside waffle cones.
7 Place cakes in cones, spread with frosting; decorate with strawberries, coconut and grated chocolate.

Butter cream frosting

Beat butter in small bowl with electric mixer until light and fluffy; beat in sifted icing sugar and milk, in two batches. Divide mixture among four small bowls. Add chopped chocolate to one and sifted cocoa to another. Using colouring, tint one pink and leave one plain.

ice-cream cone cakes

Cream cheese lemon cake

90g butter, softened
90g cream cheese, softened
2 teaspoons finely grated
    lemon rind
⅔ cup (150g) caster sugar
2 eggs
⅓ cup (50g) self-raising flour
½ cup (75g) plain flour

Meringue cases

3 egg whites
¾ cup (165g) caster sugar
1 tablespoon cornflour
1 teaspoon white vinegar
½ teaspoon vanilla extract

Decorations

300ml whipping cream,
    whipped
125g strawberries, quartered
1 tablespoon passionfruit pulp
½ cup (75g) blueberries
1 medium banana (230g),
    sliced thickly

1 Make meringue cases.
2 Preheat oven to moderate (180°C/160°C fan-assisted). Line 6-hole large or 12-hole standard muffin tray with paper cases.
3 Beat butter, cheese, rind, sugar and eggs in small bowl with electric mixer until light and fluffy.
4 Add flours to cheese mixture; beat on low speed until combined. Divide mixture among cases; smooth surface.
5 Bake large cakes about 30 minutes, small cakes about 20 minutes. Turn cakes onto wire rack to cool.
6 Drop a teaspoon of whipped cream on each cake; top with meringue cases. Spoon remaining cream into cases and decorate with fruit.

Meringue cases

Preheat oven to very low (120°C/100°C fan-assisted). Grease oven tray; line base with baking parchment, trace six 8.5cm circles onto paper for large cakes, and 12 x 5.5cm circles for small cakes. Beat egg whites in small bowl with electric mixer until soft peaks form. Gradually add sugar, a tablespoon at a time, beating until sugar dissolves between additions. Fold in cornflour, vinegar and extract. Spoon meringue inside circles on tray; hollow out slightly. Bake 45 minutes or until cases are firm. Cool in oven with door ajar.

lemon pavlova puffs

choc-mint mousse cakes

Double chocolate mint cake

125g box (16) square after
    dinner mints
60g dark eating chocolate,
    chopped coarsely
⅔ cup (160ml) water
90g butter, softened
½ teaspoon peppermint essence
1 cup (220g) firmly packed
    brown sugar
2 eggs
⅔ cup (100g) self-raising flour
2 tablespoons cocoa powder
⅓ cup (40g) ground almonds
1 tablespoon cocoa powder,
    extra

Chocolate mousse

150g dark eating chocolate,
    chopped roughly
½ teaspoon peppermint essence
¾ cup (180ml) whipping cream
2 eggs, separated
2 tablespoons caster sugar

1 Make chocolate mousse.
2 Preheat oven to moderately
low (170°C/150°C fan-assisted).
Line 6-hole large or 12-hole
standard muffin tray with
paper cases.
3 For large cakes, using a 3.5cm
long petal cutter, cut out 2 petals
from each after dinner mint. For
small cakes use a 1cm long petal
cutter, to cut 4 petals from each
after dinner mint. Coarsely chop
off-cuts, reserve for cake mixture.
4 Combine chocolate and the
water in small saucepan; stir over
low heat until smooth.
5 Beat butter, essence, sugar and
eggs in small bowl with electric
mixer until light and fluffy.
6 Stir in sifted flour and cocoa,
ground almonds, warm chocolate
mixture and reserved after
dinner mints. Divide mixture
among cases; smooth surface.
7 Bake large cakes about
40 minutes, small cakes about
30 minutes. Turn cakes onto
wire rack to cool.
8 Place a lightly greased collar
of foil around each cake. Divide
firm chocolate mousse evenly
among tops of cakes. Freeze
cakes for about 30 minutes to
help set the mousse quickly.

9 Dust mousse with extra sifted
cocoa; arrange petals on top in
a flower. Gently remove foil; dip
spatula in hot water and smooth
side of mousse.

Chocolate mousse

Combine chocolate, peppermint
essence and half the cream in a
medium heatproof bowl over a
medium saucepan of simmering
water; stir until smooth. Cool
mixture 5 minutes, then stir in
egg yolks. Beat remaining cream
in small bowl with electric mixer
until soft peaks form. Beat egg
whites in another small bowl
with electric mixer until soft
peaks form; add sugar gradually,
beat until dissolved. Fold cream
into chocolate mixture, then
egg whites. Spoon mixture into
a shallow baking dish. Cover,
refrigerate 4 hours or until firm.

sugar & lace

Caramel mud cake

125g butter, chopped coarsely
100g white eating chocolate,
  chopped coarsely
⅔ cup (150g) firmly packed
  brown sugar
¼ cup (90g) golden syrup
⅔ cup (160ml) milk
1 cup (150g) plain flour
⅓ cup (50g) self-raising flour
1 egg

Decorations

doily, lace or stencil
½ cup (80g) icing sugar

1 Preheat oven to moderately low (170°C/150°C fan-assisted). Line 6-hole large or 12-hole standard muffin tray with paper cases.
2 Combine butter, chocolate, sugar, syrup and milk in small saucepan; stir over low heat, until smooth. Transfer mixture to medium bowl; cool 15 minutes.
3 Whisk sifted flours into chocolate mixture, then egg. Divide mixture among cases.
4 Bake large cakes about 40 minutes, small cakes about 30 minutes. Turn cakes onto wire rack to cool.
5 Place doily, lace or stencil over cake; sift a little icing sugar over doily (see page 124), then carefully lift doily from cake. Repeat with remaining cakes and icing sugar.

cloud cakes

Strawberry swirl buttercake

90g butter, softened
½ teaspoon vanilla extract
½ cup (110g) caster sugar
2 eggs
1 cup (150g) self-raising flour
2 tablespoons milk
2 tablespoons strawberry jam

Fluffy frosting

1 cup (220g) caster sugar
⅓ cup (80ml) water
2 egg whites

Decorations

pink coloured sugar
   (see page 125)

1 Preheat oven to moderate (180°C/160°C fan-assisted). Line 6-hole large or 12-hole standard muffin tray with paper cases.
2 Beat butter, vanilla extract, sugar, eggs, flour and milk in small bowl with electric mixer on low speed until ingredients are just combined. Increase speed to medium, beat until mixture is changed to a paler colour.
3 Divide mixture among cases; smooth surface. Divide jam over tops of cakes; using a skewer swirl jam into cakes.
4 Bake large cakes about 30 minutes, small cakes about 20 minutes. Turn cakes onto wire rack to cool.
5 Make fluffy frosting.
6 Spread cakes with fluffy frosting; sprinkle with coloured sugar.

Fluffy frosting

Combine sugar and the water in small saucepan; stir over heat, without boiling, until sugar is dissolved. Boil, uncovered, without stirring about 5 minutes or until syrup reaches 116°C on a sugar thermometer. Syrup should be thick but not coloured. Remove from heat, allow bubbles to subside. Beat egg whites in small bowl with electric mixer until soft peaks form. While mixer is operating, add hot syrup in thin stream; beat on high speed about 10 minutes or until mixture is thick and cool.

toffee-apple towers

Maple, pecan and apple cake
60g butter, softened
1 cup (150g) self-raising flour
1 teaspoon ground cinnamon
½ cup (110g) firmly packed
  brown sugar
¼ cup (60ml) maple-flavoured
  syrup
2 eggs
⅔ cup (80g) coarsely chopped
  pecans
½ cup (85g) coarsely grated
  apple

Maple frosting
90g butter, softened
1 cup (160g) icing sugar
2 teaspoons maple-flavoured
  syrup

Toffee
1 cup (220g) caster sugar
½ cup (125ml) water

1 Preheat oven to moderate
(180°C/160°C fan-assisted). Line
6-hole large or 12-hole standard
muffin tray with paper cases.
2 Beat butter, flour, cinnamon,
sugar, syrup and eggs in small
bowl with electric mixer on low
speed until ingredients are
combined. Increase speed to
medium, beat until mixture is
changed to a paler colour.
3 Stir in nuts and grated apple.
Divide mixture among cases;
smooth surface.
4 Bake large cakes about
35 minutes, small cakes about
25 minutes. Turn cakes onto
wire rack to cool.
5 Make maple frosting.
Make toffee.
6 Spread cakes with frosting;
decorate with toffee shards.

Maple frosting
Beat butter, sifted icing sugar
and syrup in small bowl with
electric mixer until light and fluffy.

Toffee
Combine sugar with the water
in small heavy-based saucepan.
Stir over heat, without boiling,
until sugar dissolves; bring to
the boil. Reduce heat; simmer,
uncovered, without stirring,
until mixture is golden brown.
Remove from heat; stand until
bubbles subside. Make toffee
shards on baking parchment-
lined oven tray (see page 119).

turkish delights

White chocolate pistachio cake

60g white eating chocolate, chopped roughly
2 tablespoons rose water
½ cup (125ml) water
⅓ cup (45g) pistachio nuts
90g butter, softened
1 cup (220g) firmly packed brown sugar
2 eggs
⅔ cup (100g) self-raising flour
2 tablespoons plain flour

Decorations

⅔ cup (90g) coarsely chopped pistachio nuts
300g white eating chocolate, melted
900g turkish delight, chopped

1 Preheat oven to moderate (180°C/160°C fan-assisted). Line 6-hole large or 12-hole standard muffin tray with paper cases.
2 Combine chocolate, rose water and the water in small saucepan; stir over low heat until smooth.
3 Blend or process nuts until fine.
4 Beat butter, sugar and eggs in small bowl with electric mixer until combined.
5 Fold in sifted flours, ground pistachios and warm chocolate mixture. Divide among cases.
6 Bake large cakes about 35 minutes, small cakes about 25 minutes. Turn cakes onto wire rack to cool.
7 Cut a 3cm deep hole in the centre of each cake; fill with a few chopped nuts. Drizzle with a little chocolate; replace lids.
8 Decorate cakes with pieces of turkish delight and chopped nuts dipped in chocolate.

rocky road cakes

Marble cake

125g butter, softened
½ teaspoon vanilla extract
⅔ cup (150g) caster sugar
2 eggs
1¼ cups (185g) self-raising flour
⅓ cup (80ml) milk
pink food colouring
1 tablespoon cocoa powder
2 teaspoons milk, extra

Rocky road topping

½ cup (70g) unsalted roasted
   peanuts
1 cup (200g) red glacé cherries,
   halved
1 cup (100g) pink and white
   marshmallows, chopped
   coarsely
½ cup (25g) coconut flakes,
   toasted
200g milk eating chocolate,
   melted

Decorations

50g milk eating chocolate,
   melted

1 Preheat oven to moderate (180°C/160°C fan-assisted). Line 6-hole large or 12-hole standard muffin tray with paper cases.

2 Beat butter, extract, sugar and eggs in small bowl with electric mixer until light and fluffy. Stir in sifted flour and milk in two batches.

3 Divide mixture evenly among three bowls. Tint one mixture pink. Blend sifted cocoa with extra milk in cup; stir into another mixture. Leave third mixture plain.

4 Drop alternate spoonfuls of the mixtures into cases. Pull a skewer backwards and forwards through mixtures for a marbled effect; smooth surface.

5 Bake large cakes about 30 minutes, small cakes about 20 minutes. Turn cakes onto wire rack to cool.

6 Combine ingredients for rocky road topping in medium bowl.

7 Place topping on tops of cakes; drizzle with melted chocolate.

choconut angels

Vanilla buttercake

90g butter, softened
½ teaspoon vanilla extract
½ cup (110g) caster sugar
2 eggs
1 cup (150g) self-raising flour
2 tablespoons milk

Chocolate icing

10g butter
⅓ cup (80ml) milk
2 cups (320g) icing sugar
¼ cup (25g) cocoa powder

Decorations

1 cup (80g) desiccated coconut
¼ cup (100g) raspberry jam
½ cup (125ml) whipping cream,
  whipped

1 Preheat oven to moderate (180°C/160°C fan-assisted). Line 6-hole large or 12-hole standard muffin tray with paper cases.
2 Beat butter, extract, sugar, eggs, flour and milk in small bowl with electric mixer on low speed until ingredients are just combined. Increase speed to medium, beat until mixture is changed to a paler colour.
3 Divide mixture among cases; smooth surface.
4 Bake large cakes about 25 minutes, small cakes about 20 minutes. Turn cakes onto wire rack to cool.
5 Make chocolate icing.
6 Remove cases from cakes. Dip cakes in icing; drain off excess, toss cakes in coconut. Place cakes on wire rack to set.
7 Cut cakes as desired; fill with jam and cream.

Chocolate icing

Melt butter in medium heatproof bowl over medium saucepan of simmering water. Stir in milk and sifted icing sugar and cocoa until icing is a coating consistency.

Ginger buttermilk cake

½ cup (110g) firmly packed
　brown sugar
½ cup (75g) plain flour
½ cup (75g) self-raising flour
¼ teaspoon bicarbonate of soda
1 teaspoon ground ginger
½ teaspoon ground cinnamon
¼ teaspoon ground nutmeg
90g butter, softened
1 egg
¼ cup (60ml) buttermilk
2 tablespoons golden syrup

Decorations

½ cup (80g) icing sugar
400g white prepared fondant
　icing
⅓ cup (110g) ginger marmalade,
　warmed, strained
50g red prepared fondant icing
50g black prepared fondant
　icing

1 Preheat oven to moderately low (170°C/150°C fan-assisted). Line 6-hole large or 12-hole standard muffin tray with paper cases.

2 Sift dry ingredients into small bowl, then add remaining ingredients. Beat mixture with electric mixer on low speed until ingredients are combined. Increase speed to medium, beat until mixture is changed to a paler colour.

3 Divide mixture among cases; smooth surface.

4 Bake large cakes about 40 minutes, small cakes about 30 minutes. Turn cakes onto wire rack to cool.

5 Dust surface with sifted icing sugar; knead white prepared fondant icing until smooth. Roll out fondant to a thickness of 5mm. Cut out rounds large enough to cover tops of cakes.

6 Brush tops of cakes with marmalade; cover with fondant rounds (see page 120).

7 Roll out red and black fondant icing, separately, until 5mm thick. Cut out shapes using heart, diamond, club and spade cutters (see page 115).

8 Roll out red and black fondant scraps, separately, to a thickness of 2mm. Cut out 'A's using an alphabet cutter set (see page 115).

9 Secure fondant shapes to cakes by brushing backs with a tiny amount of water.

sweet ginger aces

coconut kisses

125g butter, chopped coarsely
80g white eating chocolate,
    chopped coarsely
1 cup (220g) caster sugar
½ cup (125ml) milk
½ cup (75g) plain flour
½ cup (75g) self-raising flour
½ teaspoon coconut essence
1 egg

Whipped white
chocolate ganache

¼ cup (60ml) double cream
185g white eating chocolate,
    chopped coarsely
1 tablespoon coconut liqueur

Decorations

3 x 150g boxes Ferrero
    Raffaello pralines

1 Preheat oven to moderately
low (170°C/150°C fan-assisted).
Line 6-hole large or 12-hole
standard muffin tray with
paper cases.
2 Combine butter, chocolate,
sugar and milk in small saucepan;
stir over low heat until smooth.
Transfer mixture to medium
bowl; cool 15 minutes.
3 Whisk in sifted flours, then
essence and egg. Divide mixture
among cases; smooth surface.
4 Bake large cakes about
40 minutes, small cakes about
30 minutes. Turn cakes onto
wire rack to cool.
5 Make whipped white chocolate
ganache.
6 Spread cakes with ganache.
Top with halved pralines, then
stack with whole pralines using
a little ganache to secure.

Whipped white
chocolate ganache

Bring cream to a boil in small
saucepan; pour over chocolate
and liqueur in small bowl of
electric mixer, stir until smooth.
Cover; refrigerate 30 minutes.
Beat with an electric mixer until
light and fluffy.

froufrou

Raspberry coconut cake
125g butter, softened
1 cup (220g) caster sugar
3 eggs
½ cup (75g) plain flour
¼ cup (35g) self-raising flour
½ cup (40g) desiccated coconut
⅓ cup (80g) sour cream
150g frozen raspberries

Cream cheese frosting
60g butter, softened
160g cream cheese, softened
2 teaspoons coconut essence
3 cups (480g) icing sugar

Decorations
1 cup (50g) coconut flakes,
   toasted
15 fresh raspberries, halved

1 Preheat oven to moderate
(180°C/160°C fan-assisted). Line
6-hole large or 12-hole standard
muffin tray with paper cases.
2 Beat butter, sugar and eggs
in small bowl with electric mixer
until light and fluffy.
3 Stir in sifted flours, coconut,
cream and frozen raspberries.
Divide mixture among cases;
smooth surface.
4 Bake large cakes about
50 minutes, small cakes about
40 minutes. Turn cakes onto
wire rack to cool.
5 Make cream cheese frosting.
6 Remove cases from cakes;
spread cakes with frosting.
7 Decorate cakes with coconut
and raspberries.

Cream cheese frosting
Beat butter, cream cheese and
essence in small bowl with
electric mixer until light and
fluffy; gradually beat in sifted
icing sugar.

mochaccinos

You will need six 350ml or twelve 125ml capacity coffee cups for this recipe.

Mocha mud cake

165g butter, chopped coarsely
100g dark eating chocolate, chopped coarsely
1⅓ cups (290g) caster sugar
⅔ cup (170ml) water
¼ cup (60ml) coffee liqueur
2 tablespoons instant coffee granules
1 cup (150g) plain flour
2 tablespoons self-raising flour
2 tablespoons cocoa powder
1 egg

Decorations

300ml whipping cream, whipped
2 tablespoons chocolate-flavoured topping
1 tablespoon cocoa powder

1 Preheat oven to moderately low (170°C/150°C fan-assisted). Line 6-hole large or 12-hole standard muffin tray with paper cases.
2 Combine butter, chocolate, sugar, the water, liqueur and coffee in small saucepan; stir over low heat until smooth.
3 Transfer mixture to medium bowl; cool 15 minutes. Whisk in sifted flours and cocoa, then egg. Divide mixture among cases.
4 Bake large cakes about 1 hour, small cakes about 50 minutes. Turn cakes onto wire rack to cool.
5 Remove cases from cakes. Place cakes in coffee cups, top with cream. Place chocolate topping into piping bag fitted with small plain tube, pipe spirals over cream; feather and fan cakes by pulling a skewer through the spirals (see page 124), or dust cakes with sifted cocoa.

life's a beach at 30

We used scrap book decorations available from craft shops and some newsagents. This cake can be assembled directly onto a table or covered 60cm square cake board.

Lime coconut cake
250g butter, softened
2 teaspoons coconut essence
1 tablespoon finely grated
    lime rind
1⅓ cups (290g) caster sugar
4 eggs
⅔ cup (160ml) milk
1½ cups (120g) desiccated
    coconut
2½ cups (375g) self-raising flour

Coconut cream cheese frosting
60g butter, softened
160g cream cheese, softened
2 teaspoons coconut essence
3 cups (480g) icing sugar

Decorations
60g plain sweet biscuits,
    crushed finely
beach-themed decorations

1 Preheat oven to moderate (180°C/160°C fan-assisted). Line two 12-hole standard muffin trays with paper cases.
2 Beat butter, essence, rind, sugar and eggs in large bowl with electric mixer until combined.
3 Stir in milk and coconut, then sifted flour. Divide mixture among cases; smooth surface.
4 Bake cakes about 25 minutes. Turn cakes onto wire rack to cool.
5 Make coconut cream cheese frosting.
6 Cover backs of decorations with baking paper to prevent them staining.
7 Spread cakes with frosting; dip tops of cakes into biscuit crumbs, top with decorations.

Coconut cream cheese frosting
Beat butter, cream cheese and essence in small bowl with electric mixer until light and fluffy; gradually beat in sifted icing sugar.

florentine cakes

Double chocolate mud cake

60g dark eating chocolate,
  chopped coarsely
⅔ cup (160ml) water
90g butter, softened
1 cup (220g) firmly packed
  brown sugar
2 eggs
⅔ cup (100g) self-raising flour
2 tablespoons cocoa powder
⅓ cup (40g) ground almonds

Milk chocolate ganache

100g milk eating chocolate,
  chopped coarsely
¼ cup (60ml) double cream

Florentine topping

1 cup (80g) flaked almonds,
  toasted
½ cup (115g) coarsely chopped
  glacé ginger
1 cup (200g) red glacé cherries,
  halved

Decorations

50g dark eating chocolate,
  melted

1 Preheat oven to moderately
low (170°C/150°C fan-assisted).
Line 6-hole large or 12-hole
standard muffin tray with
paper cases.
2 Combine chocolate and the
water in small saucepan; stir
over low heat until smooth.
3 Beat butter, sugar and eggs
in small bowl with electric mixer
until light and fluffy.
4 Stir in sifted flour and cocoa,
ground almonds and warm
chocolate mixture. Divide
mixture among cases; smooth
surface.
5 Bake large cakes about
35 minutes, small cakes about
25 minutes. Turn cakes onto
wire rack to cool.
6 Make milk chocolate ganache.
7 Combine ingredients for
florentine topping in small bowl.
8 Spread cakes with ganache,
top with florentine mixture;
drizzle with chocolate.

Milk chocolate ganache
Bring cream to a boil in small
saucepan, pour over chocolate
in small bowl; stir until smooth.
Stand at room temperature
until ganache is spreadable.

baby blue

Choc-orange almond cake

60g dark eating chocolate,
  chopped coarsely
1 teaspoon finely grated
  orange rind
⅔ cup (160ml) orange juice
90g butter, softened
1 cup (220g) firmly packed
  brown sugar
2 eggs
⅔ cup (100g) self-raising flour
2 tablespoons cocoa powder
⅓ cup (40g) ground almonds

Decorations

½ cup (80g) icing sugar
400g white prepared fondant
  icing
blue food colouring
⅓ cup (110g) orange marmalade,
  warmed, sieved
2m ribbon, approximately

1 Preheat oven to moderately
low (170°C/150°C fan-assisted).
Line 6-hole large or 12-hole
standard muffin tray with
paper cases.
2 Combine chocolate, rind and
juice in small saucepan; stir over
low heat until smooth.
3 Beat butter, sugar and eggs
in small bowl with electric mixer
until light and fluffy.
4 Stir in sifted flour and cocoa,
ground almonds and warm
chocolate mixture. Divide mixture
among cases; smooth surface.
5 Bake large cakes about
35 minutes, small cakes about
25 minutes. Turn cakes onto
wire rack to cool.
6 Dust surface with sifted icing
sugar, knead fondant icing until
smooth. Knead blue colouring
into icing (see page 120).
7 Brush tops of cakes with
marmalade. Roll fondant out to
5mm thickness; cut rounds large
enough to cover tops of cakes.
8 Place rounds on cakes; tie
cakes with ribbon.

tiramisu

Vanilla buttercake

90g butter, softened
½ teaspoon vanilla extract
½ cup (110g) caster sugar
2 eggs
1 cup (150g) self-raising flour
2 tablespoons milk

Mascarpone cream

250g mascarpone cheese
¼ cup (40g) icing sugar
1 tablespoon marsala
¾ cup (180ml) whipping cream,
  whipped

Coffee mixture

1 tablespoon instant coffee
  granules
⅓ cup (80ml) boiling water
2 tablespoons marsala

Decorations

50g dark eating chocolate,
  grated finely

1 Preheat oven to moderate (180°C/160°C fan-assisted). Line 6-hole large or 12-hole standard muffin tray with paper cases.
2 Beat butter, extract, sugar, eggs, flour and milk in small bowl with electric mixer on low speed until ingredients are just combined. Increase speed to medium, beat until mixture is changed to a paler colour. Divide mixture among cases; smooth surface.
3 Bake large cakes about 25 minutes, small cakes about 20 minutes. Turn cakes onto wire rack to cool.
4 Make mascarpone cream. Make coffee mixture.
5 Remove cases from cakes. Cut each cake horizontally into four. Brush both sides of cake slices with coffee mixture. Join cake slices with mascarpone cream.
6 Spread tops of cakes with mascarpone cream; sprinkle with grated chocolate. Refrigerate for 3 hours before serving.

Mascarpone cream

Combine mascarpone, sifted icing sugar and marsala in small bowl; fold in cream.

Coffee mixture

Combine coffee, the water and marsala in small bowl; cool.

lemon cheesecakes

Lemon cheesecake

100g sweet digestive biscuits
50g butter, melted
2 x 250g packets cream cheese, softened
2 teaspoons finely grated lemon rind
½ cup (110g) caster sugar
2 eggs

Glaze

⅔ cup (220g) apricot jam
2 tablespoons brandy

1 Preheat oven to low (150°C/130°C fan-assisted). Line 6-hole large or 12-hole standard muffin tray with paper cases.

2 Blend or process biscuits until fine. Add butter; process until just combined. Divide mixture among cases; press firmly. Refrigerate 30 minutes.

3 Beat cheese, rind and sugar in small bowl with electric mixer until smooth. Beat in eggs. Pour mixture into cases.

4 Bake large cakes about 30 minutes, small cakes about 25 minutes. Cool.

5 Make glaze.

6 Pour glaze evenly over tops of cheesecakes; refrigerate 2 hours or until glaze is set.

Glaze

Heat jam and brandy in small saucepan over low heat; sieve.

125g butter, softened
½ teaspoon vanilla extract
⅔ cup (150g) caster sugar
2 eggs
¾ cup (150g) finely chopped
   dried figs
½ cup (60g) finely chopped
   walnuts
⅔ cup (100g) plain flour
⅓ cup (50g) self-raising flour
60g Mars bar, chopped finely
¼ cup (60ml) milk

⅓ cup (80ml) double cream
200g milk eating chocolate

½ cup (110g) caster sugar
¼ cup (60ml) water

6 medium fresh figs (360g),
   quartered

1 Preheat oven to moderate (180°C/160°C fan-assisted). Line 6-hole large or 12-hole standard muffin tray with paper cases.
2 Beat butter, extract, sugar and eggs in small bowl with electric mixer until light and fluffy.
3 Stir in figs, nuts, sifted flours, Mars bar and milk. Divide mixture among cases; smooth surface.
4 Bake large cakes about 40 minutes, small cakes about 30 minutes. Turn cakes onto wire rack to cool.
5 Make whipped milk chocolate ganache.
6 Make toffee; form into shapes over rolling pin (see page 119).
7 Spread cakes with ganache; decorate with fig quarters and toffee shapes.

Bring cream to a boil in small saucepan, pour over chocolate in small bowl of electric mixer, stir until smooth. Cover, refrigerate for 30 minutes. Beat with electric mixer until light and fluffy.

Combine sugar with the water in small heavy-based saucepan. Stir over heat, without boiling, until sugar dissolves; bring to the boil. Reduce heat; simmer, uncovered, without stirring, until mixture is golden brown. Remove from heat; stand until bubbles subside.

fig and toffee crowns

orange blossom cakes

Orange, almond and cranberry cake
125g butter, softened
2 teaspoons finely grated orange rind
⅔ cup (150g) caster sugar
2 eggs
1 cup (150g) self-raising flour
⅓ cup (50g) plain flour
⅓ cup (40g) ground almonds
½ cup (65g) dried cranberries
¼ cup (60ml) orange juice
2 tablespoons milk

Modelling fondant
2 teaspoons gelatine
1½ tablespoons water
2 teaspoons glucose syrup
1½ cups (240g) icing sugar
½ cup (80g) icing sugar, extra
yellow, orange and pink food colouring

Butter cream
90g butter, softened
¼ teaspoon orange essence
1 cup (160g) icing sugar
1 tablespoon milk
yellow, orange and pink food colouring

1 Make modelling fondant; reserve a walnut-sized portion.
2 Dust surface with icing sugar, roll remaining fondant to a thickness of approximately 3mm. Cut out 18 flowers using 3cm cutter or 36 flowers using 2cm cutter (see page 115).
3 Divide reserved fondant into three; knead one of the colourings into each portion. Roll tiny balls for flower centres; lightly brush flower centres with water to secure coloured balls.
4 Preheat oven to moderate (180°C/160°C fan-assisted). Line 6-hole large or 12-hole standard muffin tray with paper cases.
5 Beat butter, rind, sugar and eggs in small bowl with electric mixer until light and fluffy.
6 Stir in sifted flours, ground almonds, cranberries, juice and milk. Divide mixture among cases; smooth surface.
7 Bake large cakes about 35 minutes, small cakes about 25 minutes. Turn cakes onto wire rack to cool.
8 Make butter cream.
9 Spread cakes with butter cream; decorate with flowers.

Modelling fondant
Sprinkle gelatine over the water in cup; stand cup in small saucepan of simmering water, stirring until gelatine is dissolved, add glucose. Place half the sifted icing sugar in small bowl, stir in gelatine mixture. Gradually stir in remaining sifted icing sugar, knead on surface dusted with extra sifted icing sugar until smooth. Enclose in cling film.

Butter cream
Beat butter and essence in small bowl with electric mixer until light and fluffy. Beat in sifted icing sugar and milk, in two batches. Beat in a little of the desired colouring.

neapolitan cakes

Marbled buttercake

125g butter, softened
½ teaspoon vanilla extract
⅔ cup (150g) caster sugar
2 eggs
1¼ cups (185g) self-raising flour
⅓ cup (80ml) milk
pink food colouring
1 tablespoon cocoa powder
2 teaspoons milk, extra

Butter cream

125g butter, softened
1½ cups (240g) icing sugar
2 tablespoons milk
pink food colouring
1 tablespoon cocoa powder
2 teaspoons milk, extra

1 Preheat oven to moderate (180°C/160°C fan-assisted). Line 6-hole large or 12-hole standard muffin tray with paper cases.
2 Beat butter, extract, sugar and eggs in small bowl with electric mixer until light and fluffy. Stir in sifted flour and milk, in two batches.
3 Divide mixture evenly among three bowls. Tint one mixture pink. Blend sifted cocoa with extra milk in cup; stir into another mixture. Leave third mixture plain.
4 Drop alternate spoonfuls of the three mixtures into cases. Pull a skewer backwards and forwards through mixtures for a marbled effect; smooth surface.
5 Bake large cakes about 30 minutes, small cakes about 20 minutes. Turn cakes onto wire rack to cool.
6 Make butter cream.
7 Spread cakes with the three colours of butter cream.

Butter cream

Beat butter in small bowl with electric mixer until as white as possible; beat in sifted icing sugar and milk, in two batches. Divide mixture evenly among three bowls. Tint one mixture pink. Blend sifted cocoa with extra milk in cup; stir into another mixture. Leave third mixture plain.

kaleidocakes

Orange buttercake

90g butter, softened
90g cream cheese, softened
2 teaspoons finely grated
    orange rind
⅔ cup (150g) caster sugar
2 eggs
⅓ cup (50g) self-raising flour
½ cup (75g) plain flour

Fondant icing

300g white prepared fondant
    icing, chopped coarsely
1 egg white
¼ teaspoon orange essence

Royal icing

1½ cups (240g) icing sugar
1 egg white
½ teaspoon lemon juice
yellow, orange, green, pink and
    purple food colouring

1 Preheat oven to moderate
(180°C/160°C fan-assisted). Line
6-hole large or 12-hole standard
muffin tray with paper cases.
2 Beat butter, cheese, rind, sugar
and eggs in small bowl with
electric mixer until light and fluffy.
3 Beat in flours on low speed until
just combined. Divide mixture
among cases; smooth surface.
4 Bake large cakes about
30 minutes, small cakes about
20 minutes. Turn cakes onto
wire rack to cool.
5 Make fondant icing. Spread
over cakes; allow to set at
room temperature.
6 Make royal icing. Divide evenly
among five small bowls. Using
colourings, tint icing yellow,
orange, green, pink and purple;
cover each tightly with cling film.
Pipe patterns (see page 122)
using picture as a guide.

Fondant icing

Place icing in a small bowl over
a small saucepan of simmering
water; stir until smooth. Stir in
egg white and essence. Stand at
room temperature for 10 minutes
or until thickened slightly. Spread
fondant quickly over cakes; use
a metal spatula dipped in hot
water to smooth surface.

Royal icing

Sift icing sugar through very fine
sieve. Lightly beat egg white in
small bowl with electric mixer;
add icing sugar, a tablespoon at
a time. When icing reaches firm
peaks, use a wooden spoon to
beat in juice; cover tightly with
cling film.

banana caramel cakes

90g butter, softened
½ cup (110g) firmly packed
   brown sugar
2 eggs
½ cup (75g) self-raising flour
½ cup (75g) plain flour
½ teaspoon bicarbonate
   of soda
½ teaspoon mixed spice
⅔ cup mashed overripe banana
⅓ cup (80g) sour cream
2 tablespoons milk

Filling and decorations

380g dulce de leche (caramel
   sauce)
½ cup (125ml) whipping cream,
   whipped
2 medium bananas (400g),
   sliced thinly
100g dark eating chocolate

1 Preheat oven to moderate
(180°C/160°C fan-assisted). Line
6-hole large or 12-hole standard
muffin tray with paper cases.
2 Beat butter, sugar and eggs
in small bowl with electric mixer
until light and fluffy.
3 Stir in sifted dry ingredients,
banana, sour cream and milk.
Divide mixture among cases;
smooth surface.
4 Bake large cakes about
25 minutes, small cakes about
20 minutes. Turn cakes onto
wire rack to cool.
5 Remove cases from cakes.
6 Fold 2 tablespoons of the
caramel sauce into cream.
7 Cut cakes horizontally into
three slices. Re-assemble cakes
with remaining caramel and
banana. Top cakes with caramel-
flavoured cream.
8 Using a vegetable peeler,
grate chocolate (see page 116);
sprinkle over cakes.

lemon meringue cakes

Coconut lemon curd cake

125g butter, softened
2 teaspoons finely grated
   lemon rind
⅔ cup (150g) caster sugar
2 eggs
⅓ cup (80ml) milk
¾ cup (60g) desiccated coconut
1¼ cups (185g) self-raising flour

Lemon curd

4 egg yolks
⅓ cup (75g) caster sugar
2 teaspoons finely grated
   lemon rind
¼ cup (60ml) lemon juice
40g butter

Coconut meringue

4 egg whites
1 cup (220g) caster sugar
1⅓ cups (95g) shredded
   coconut, chopped finely

1 Make lemon curd.
2 Preheat oven to moderate (180°C/160°C fan-assisted). Line 6-hole large or 12-hole standard muffin tray with paper cases.
3 Beat butter, rind, sugar and eggs in small bowl with electric mixer until light and fluffy.
4 Stir in milk and coconut, then sifted flour. Divide mixture among cases; smooth surface.
5 Bake large cakes about 25 minutes, small cakes about 20 minutes. Turn cakes onto wire rack to cool. Increase oven to hot (220°C/200°C fan-assisted).
6 Cut a 2cm-deep hole in the centre of each cake, fill with curd; discard cake tops.
7 Make coconut meringue; spoon into a piping bag fitted with a 1cm plain tube.
8 Pipe meringue on top of each cake (see page 122); place cakes on oven tray.
9 Bake in hot oven 5 minutes or until meringue is browned lightly.

Lemon curd

Combine ingredients in a small heatproof bowl over small saucepan of simmering water, stirring constantly, until mixture thickens slightly and coats the back of a spoon. Remove from heat. Cover tightly; refrigerate lemon curd until cold.

Coconut meringue

Beat egg whites in small bowl with electric mixer until soft peaks form; gradually add sugar, beating until sugar dissolves. Fold in coconut.

sweetheart

Raspberry swirl cake

125g butter, softened
½ teaspoon vanilla extract
⅔ cup (150g) caster sugar
2 eggs
1¼ cups (185g) self-raising flour
⅓ cup (80ml) milk
pink food colouring
2 tablespoons raspberry jam

Decorations

½ cup (80g) icing sugar
350g white prepared fondant
   icing
⅓ cup (110g) raspberry jam,
   warmed, sieved
¼ teaspoon vodka
¼ teaspoon pink petal dust

1 Preheat oven to moderate (180°C/160°C fan-assisted). Line 6-hole large or 12-hole standard muffin tray with paper cases.

2 Beat butter, extract, sugar and eggs in small bowl with electric mixer until light and fluffy. Stir in sifted flour and milk, in two batches.

3 Divide mixture evenly between two bowls. Tint one mixture pink; leave other mixture plain. Drop alternate spoonfuls of the two mixtures into cases.

4 Divide jam among cakes, pull a skewer backwards and forwards through mixtures for a swirling effect; smooth surface.

5 Bake large cakes about 30 minutes, small cakes about 20 minutes. Turn cakes onto wire rack to cool.

6 On surface dusted with sifted icing sugar, knead fondant icing until smooth. Tint fondant with pink colouring; knead into fondant only until marbled (see page 120). Roll out fondant to a thickness of 5mm. Cut out rounds large enough to cover tops of cakes.

7 Blend vodka with petal dust. Using a fine paint brush, paint mixture onto a heart-shaped rubber stamp; press lightly onto fondant rounds. Pinch edges of rounds with fingers.

8 Brush tops of cakes with jam; top with stamped rounds.

chocolate valentines

Double chocolate raspberry cake

60g dark eating chocolate, chopped coarsely
½ cup (125ml) water
90g butter, softened
1 cup (220g) firmly packed brown sugar
2 eggs
⅔ cup (100g) self-raising flour
2 tablespoons cocoa powder
⅓ cup (40g) ground almonds
100g frozen raspberries

Decorations

2 tablespoons cocoa powder
900g chocolate prepared fondant icing
⅓ cup (110g) raspberry jam, warmed, sieved
½ cup (80g) icing sugar
150g red prepared fondant icing
150g white prepared fondant icing
pink food colouring

1 Preheat oven to moderately low (170°C/150°C fan-assisted). Line 6-hole large or 12-hole standard muffin tray with paper cases.
2 Combine chocolate and the water in small saucepan; stir over low heat until smooth.
3 Beat butter, sugar and eggs in small bowl with electric mixer until just combined.
4 Stir in sifted flour and cocoa, ground almonds, then warm chocolate mixture; fold in raspberries. Divide mixture among cases; smooth surface.
5 Bake large cakes about 55 minutes, small cakes about 45 minutes. Turn cakes onto wire rack to cool.
6 Remove cases from cakes. On a surface dusted with sifted cocoa, knead chocolate fondant icing until smooth. Roll out to a thickness of 5mm. Cut out rounds large enough to cover tops of cakes.

7 Brush cakes with jam; cover cakes with chocolate fondant.
8 On a surface dusted with sifted icing sugar, knead white and red fondant icing separately until smooth. Use colouring to tint 100g of the white fondant pink and remaining white fondant a paler pink.
9 Roll each coloured fondant icing to a thickness of 5mm. Using heart-shaped cutters of varying sizes (see page 115) to suit size of cakes, cut out hearts from fondants using picture as a guide.
10 Decorate cakes with fondant hearts, each brushed with a little water to secure to each other.

coconut cherry hearts

Choc-chip cherry cake

125g butter, softened
½ teaspoon coconut essence
⅔ cup (150g) caster sugar
2 eggs
⅓ cup (80ml) milk
½ cup (40g) desiccated coconut
⅓ cup (70g) red glacé cherries,
  chopped coarsely
50g dark eating chocolate,
  chopped coarsely
1 cup (150g) self-raising flour
¼ cup (35g) plain flour

Milk chocolate ganache

¼ cup (60ml) double cream
100g milk eating chocolate,
  chopped coarsely

Decorations

150g white eating chocolate,
  melted
pink food colouring

1 Preheat oven to moderate (180°C/160°C fan-assisted). Line 6-hole large or 12-hole standard muffin tray with paper cases.
2 Beat butter, essence, sugar and eggs in small bowl with electric mixer until combined.
3 Stir in milk, coconut, cherries and chocolate, then sifted flours. Divide mixture among cases; smooth surface.
4 Bake large cakes about 35 minutes, small cakes about 25 minutes. Turn cakes onto wire rack to cool.
5 Make milk chocolate ganache.
6 Divide white chocolate evenly among three small bowls; tint two portions with two different shades of pink (see page 117).
7 Make three paper piping bags (see page 117); spoon a different coloured chocolate mixture into each bag. Pipe different coloured heart shapes in varying sizes (see page 117), onto baking paper-lined oven tray. Set at room temperature.
8 Spread cakes with ganache; decorate with coloured hearts.

Milk chocolate ganache
Bring cream to a boil in small saucepan; pour over chocolate in small bowl, stir until smooth. Cover bowl; stand at room temperature until ganache is spreadable

the wedding story

It's important to measure the cake mixture carefully, so the cakes are all the same depth. Make the full amount of mixture; it will be fine standing at room temperature while you bake the 70 cakes in batches. We used standard sized foil cases. You need 64 cakes for the story board. We used scrap book decorations, available from craft and haberdashery shops and some newsagents.

White chocolate mud cake

500g butter, chopped coarsely
360g white eating chocolate, chopped coarsely
4 cups (880g) caster sugar
2 cups (500ml) milk
3 cups (450g) plain flour
1 cup (150g) self-raising flour
2 teaspoons vanilla extract
4 eggs

Fluffy mock cream frosting

2 tablespoons milk
⅓ cup (80ml) water
1 cup (220g) caster sugar
1 teaspoon gelatine
2 tablespoons water, extra
250g butter, softened
1 teaspoon vanilla extract

Royal icing

1½ cups (240g) icing sugar
1 egg white
½ teaspoon lemon juice

Decorations

60cm square cake board
wedding-themed decorations
3m silver ribbon

1 Preheat oven to moderately low (170°C/150°C fan-assisted). Line two 12-hole standard muffin trays with foil cases.
2 Stir butter, chocolate, sugar and milk in large saucepan, over low heat, until smooth. Transfer to large bowl; cool 15 minutes.
3 Whisk in sifted flours then extract and eggs. Drop exactly 2 level tablespoons of mixture into each case.
4 Bake cakes about 25 minutes. Turn onto wire rack to cool.
5 Meanwhile make fluffy mock cream frosting and royal icing. Cover backs of decorations with baking paper to prevent them from absorbing the frosting.
6 Spread 64 cakes with frosting, place on cake board. Secure ribbon around cakes.

7 Make royal icing; spoon icing into a piping bag fitted with a small plain tube. Pipe hearts onto about 10 of the cakes.
8 Top remaining cakes with wedding-themed decorations.

Fluffy mock cream frosting

Combine milk, the water and sugar in small saucepan, stir over low heat, without boiling, until sugar is dissolved. Sprinkle gelatine over extra water in cup, add to pan; stir syrup until gelatine is dissolved. Cool to room temperature. Beat butter and extract in small bowl with electic mixer, until as white as possible. While motor is operating, gradually pour in cold syrup; beat until light and fluffy. Mixture will thicken on standing.

Royal icing

Sift icing sugar through very fine sieve. Lightly beat egg white in small bowl with electric mixer; add icing sugar, a tablespoon at a time. When icing reaches firm peaks, use a wooden spoon to beat in juice; cover tightly with cling film.

wedding
gift cakes

This cake is simply a stack of boxes each containing a cupcake for your wedding guests to take home. The choice of boxes, colours of ribbon and flowers is up to you. Choose the boxes first – size, colour, and quantity. For the ribbon, measure each box, allowing enough ribbon to wrap around and overlap slightly. Our cake has been assembled directly onto a table, but you could also use a covered board. Choose flowers that complement the rest of the wedding flowers. We topped the boxes with a traditional cake for the bride and groom to cut. Alternatively, use a stunning arrangement of flowers. The first recipe explains what we did, using 54 cupcakes. This is only a guide – make the stack larger or smaller, or have more take-home boxes set aside. Most cupcake recipes in this book make 6 large or 12 standard muffin-sized cakes, you will have to work out the size, type and flavour of cake you'd like, and then work out how many batches of the recipe you'd need.

54 cupcakes
9cm square cake
10cm square cake board
400g white prepared fondant
¼ cup (100g) apricot jam, warmed, sieved
400g prepared almond paste
½ cup (80g) icing sugar
20m ribbon
54 x 8cm square gift boxes

1 Bake cupcakes for gift boxes and 9cm square cake of your choice.
2 Secure square cake to board with small piece of fondant icing made into a paste with water. Brush cake all over with jam.
3 Knead almond paste on surface dusted with sifted icing sugar, cover cake (see page 120); stand overnight.
4 Brush almond paste with jam, cover cake with fondant (see page 120); stand overnight.
5 Secure ribbon to each box with glue or sticky tape.
6 Place one cupcake in each box; stack boxes. Position square cake on top. Decorate with flowers.

These recipes are for the cake on the top tier; use your favourite. All cakes are baked in a greased and lined deep 9cm square tin. A filigree textured plate was used to mark the fondant.

rich fruit cake

60g butter, softened
⅓ cup (75g) firmly packed brown sugar
1 egg
2 teaspoons orange marmalade
375g (2⅓ cups) mixed dried fruit, chopped finely
⅓ (50g) cup plain flour
¼ cup (35g) self-raising flour
½ teaspoon mixed spice
2 tablespoons sweet sherry
2 tablespoons sweet sherry, extra

1 Preheat oven to low (150°C/ 130°C fan-assisted).

2 Follow method for Christmas snowflakes on page 111 for cake.
3 Bake cake about 2 hours.

white chocolate mud cake

60g butter, chopped coarsely
40g white chocolate, chopped coarsely
½ cup (110g) caster sugar
¼ cup (60ml) milk
⅓ cup (50g) plain flour
2 tablespoons self-raising flour
½ teaspoon vanilla extract
1 egg, beaten lightly

1 Preheat oven to moderately low (170°C/150°C fan-assisted).
2 Follow method for Coconut kisses on page 35 for this cake.
3 Bake cake about 1 hour.

dark chocolate mud cake

80g butter, chopped coarsely
50g dark chocolate, chopped coarsely
⅔ cup (150g) caster sugar
⅓ cup (80ml) hot water
2 tablespoons coffee liqueur
1 tablespoon instant coffee granules
½ cup (75g) plain flour
1 tablespoon self-raising flour
1 tablespoon cocoa powder
1 egg, beaten lightly

1 Preheat oven to moderately low (170°C/150°C fan-assisted).
2 Follow method for Florentine cakes on page 43 for this cake.
3 Bake cake about 1¾ hours.

This recipe makes three individual mini wedding cakes. Arrange the three together at different heights or levels (maybe even interwined with flowers) for a lovely effect.

White chocolate and apricot mud cake

125g butter, chopped coarsely
75g white chocolate, chopped coarsely
1 cup (220g) caster sugar
½ cup (125ml) milk
¾ cup (105g) plain flour
½ cup (75g) self-raising flour
½ cup (75g) finely chopped dried apricots
½ teaspoon vanilla extract
1 egg
⅓ cup (110g) apricot jam, warmed, sieved
½ cup (80g) icing sugar
900g white prepared fondant

Modelling fondant

2 teaspoons gelatine
1½ tablespoons water
2 teaspoons glucose syrup
1½ cups (240g) icing sugar
½ cup (80g) icing sugar, extra

Royal icing

1½ cups (240g) icing sugar
1 egg white
½ teaspoon lemon juice

1 Make modelling fondant. On a surface dusted with extra icing sugar, roll fondant to approximately 3mm thick. Cut out flowers using 3.5cm and 1.5cm cutters (see page 115). Shape flowers using a ball tool (see pages 120 and 115); dry on tea towel.
2 Preheat oven to moderately low (170°C/150°C fan-assisted). Line 6-hole large muffin tray with paper cases.
3 Combine butter, chocolate, sugar and milk in small saucepan; stir over low heat, until smooth. Transfer mixture to medium bowl; cool 15 minutes.
4 Whisk in sifted flours, apricots, then extract and egg; divide mixture among cases.
5 Bake cakes about 45 minutes. Turn cakes onto wire rack to cool.
6 Meanwhile make royal icing. Spoon icing into piping bag fitted with small plain tube, keep icing covered with a damp cloth.
7 Remove cases from cakes. Trim cake edges to make neat cylindrical shapes when stacked. Join two trimmed cakes with apricot jam; brush cakes all over with remaining jam.
8 On surface dusted with sifted icing sugar, knead fondant icing until smooth. Divide fondant

into three equal portions. Roll out each portion to a thickness of 5mm. Cover the three cake stacks individually with fondant icing. Trim bases and smooth fondant (see page 120).
9 Pipe a little royal icing onto the back of each flower; secure to cake. Pipe some dots in the centre of each flower and around the base of each cake.

Modelling fondant

Sprinkle gelatine over the water in cup; stand cup in small saucepan of simmering water, stirring until gelatine is dissolved; add glucose. Place half the sifted icing sugar in medium bowl, stir in gelatine mixture. Gradually stir in remaining sifted icing sugar. Knead on surface dusted with extra sifted icing sugar until smooth. Wrap tightly in cling film to prevent drying out.

Royal icing

Sift icing sugar through very fine sieve. Lightly beat egg white in small bowl with electric mixer; add icing sugar, a tablespoon at a time. When icing reaches firm peaks, use a wooden spoon to beat in juice; cover tightly with cling film.

white wedding

lily wedding cakes

Rich fruit cake

90g butter, softened
½ cup (110g) firmly packed
  brown sugar
2 eggs
1 tablespoon orange marmalade
500g (2¾ cups) mixed dried
  fruit, chopped finely
⅔ cup (100g) plain flour
2 tablespoons self-raising flour
1 teaspoon mixed spice
2 tablespoons sweet sherry
2 tablespoons sweet sherry, extra

Modelling fondant

2 teaspoons gelatine
1½ tablespoons water
2 teaspoons glucose syrup
1½ cups (240g) icing sugar
½ cup (80g) icing sugar, extra

Royal icing

1½ cups (240g) icing sugar
1 egg white
½ teaspoon lemon juice

Decorations

⅓ cup (110g) apricot jam,
  warmed, sieved
½ cup (80g) icing sugar
900g white prepared fondant
covered 22 gauge wire
florist tape
30 stamens

1 Make modelling fondant. On surface dusted with extra sifted icing sugar, roll a little of the fondant to approximately 2mm thick. Cut out petals using lily petal cutter (see pages 115 and 121) allowing 6 petals for each cake. Vary size of petals to suit size of cakes. Using frilling tool (see pages 115 and 121), gently shape petals; attach damp 10cm length wire to each petal (see pages 115 and 121); allow to dry (see page 121).

2 Preheat oven to low (150°C/ 130°C fan-assisted). Line 6-hole large or 12-hole standard muffin tray with paper cases.

3 Beat butter, sugar and eggs in small bowl with electric mixer until just combined.

4 Transfer mixture to medium bowl; add marmalade and fruit, mix well.

5 Sift flours and spice over mixture; add sherry, mix well. Divide mixture among cases; smooth surface.

6 Bake large cakes about 1 hour, small cakes about 50 minutes. Remove cakes from oven; brush tops with extra sherry. Cover pan tightly with foil; cool cakes in pan.

7 Meanwhile, assemble lilies using royal icing, stamens and pistles (see page 121).

8 Remove cases from cakes. Brush cakes with jam. On surface dusted with sifted icing sugar, knead prepared fondant until smooth. Divide fondant into six or 12 equal portions. Roll out each portion to a thickness of 5mm. Cover cakes with fondant icing; trim base and smooth fondant (see page 120).

9 Make royal icing. Spoon royal icing into piping bag fitted with small plain tube. Pipe a continuous line in a cornelli pattern over cakes (see page 122). Secure lilies to cakes.

Modelling fondant

Sprinkle gelatine over the water in cup; stand cup in small saucepan of simmering water, stirring until gelatine is dissolved, add glucose. Sift half the icing sugar in medium bowl, stir in gelatine mixture. Gradually stir in remaining sifted icing sugar, knead on surface dusted with extra sifted icing sugar until smooth. Wrap tightly in cling film to prevent drying out.

Royal icing

Sift icing sugar through very fine sieve. Lightly beat egg white in small bowl; add icing sugar, a tablespoon at a time, beating well after each addition. When icing reaches firm peaks, add juice; beat well. Cover tightly with cling film.

If your oven won't hold three sets of muffin pans, it's fine to leave the mixture standing at room temperature while the first batch bakes. We used three cake stands stacked on top of each other to display the cakes. They measured 17cm, 24cm and 34cm in diameter. We used a plastic filigree textured plate to mark the icing, available from craft or haberdashery shops. Mix and match the colours of the plates, cakes and flowers to suit the occasion.

Rich fruit cake

250g butter, softened
1¼ cups (250g) firmly packed
  brown sugar
4 eggs
2 tablespoons orange
  marmalade
1.5kg (7¾ cups) mixed dried
  fruit, chopped finely
1½ cups (225g) plain flour
½ cup (75g) self-raising flour
2 teaspoons mixed spice
½ cup (125ml) sweet sherry
¼ cup (30g) blanched whole
  almonds
2 tablespoons sweet sherry, extra

Decorations

½ cup (80g) icing sugar
750g white prepared fondant
filigree textured plate
½ cup (160g) orange marmalade,
  warmed, sieved
edible silver lustre

1 Preheat oven to low (150°C/ 130°C fan-assisted). Line three 12-hole standard muffin trays with silver foil and paper cases.
2 Beat butter, sugar and eggs in small bowl with electric mixer until just combined.
3 Transfer mixture to large bowl, add marmalade and fruit; mix well.
4 Sift flours and spice over mixture, add sherry; mix well.
5 Place 2 level tablespoons of mixture into each case; smooth surface.
6 Bake cakes about 50 minutes. Remove cakes from oven; brush tops with extra sherry. Cover pan tightly with foil; cool cakes in pan.
7 On surface dusted with sifted icing sugar, knead fondant until smooth. Roll out to a thickness of 5mm. Using a 7cm round fluted cutter cut out 36 rounds.
8 Using a filigree textured plate (see page 115), gently press an imprint onto each fondant round (see page 125).
9 Brush cakes with marmalade; top with fondant rounds. Carefully brush silver lustre over pattern on fondant.

lace wedding cakes

deluxe chocolate wedding

You need to buy triple the quantity of the ingredients for the cake recipe below. You will need to make three separate batches, do not double or triple this recipe. It's important to measure the cake mixture carefully so the cakes are all the same depth. The mixture will be fine standing at room temperature while you bake the cakes in batches. Each batch will make 40 cakes. You need 120 standard muffin paper cases.

Mocha mud cake

500g butter, chopped coarsely
300g dark eating chocolate, chopped coarsely
4 cups (880g) caster sugar
2 cups (500ml) water
⅔ cup (160ml) coffee liqueur
2 tablespoons instant coffee granules
3 cups (450g) plain flour
½ cup (75g) self-raising flour
½ cup (50g) cocoa powder
4 eggs

Dark chocolate ganache

600ml whipping cream
800g dark eating chocolate, chopped coarsely

Decorations

15cm, 20cm, 30cm, 35cm and 45cm round boards
5m x 1.5cm cotton lace ribbon
4 empty cans, 9cm tall and 5cm in diameter
wrapping paper, for cans
200g milk eating chocolate
½ cup (115g) finely chopped glacé ginger
½ cup (10g) dried rose petals
¼ cup (25g) roasted coffee beans
2 miniature brandy snaps

1 Preheat oven to moderately low (170°C/150°C fan-assisted). Line two 12-hole standard muffin trays with paper cases.
2 Combine butter, chocolate, sugar, the water, liqueur and coffee in large saucepan; stir over low heat until smooth. Transfer mixture to large bowl; cool 15 minutes.
3 Whisk in sifted flours and cocoa, then eggs. Pour exactly ¼ cup of mixture into each case.

4 Bake cakes about 40 minutes. Turn cakes onto wire racks to cool.
5 Make dark chocolate ganache.
6 Attach ribbon to edge of round boards, using double sided tape. Cover cans with wrapping paper. Glue cans to centre of the four largest boards. Stack boards from the bottom tier up, as shown in picture.
7 Spread all cakes with ganache. Decorate cakes as shown with chocolate curls using vegetable peeler (see page 116), glacé ginger, coffee beans, rose petals and brandy snaps.
8 Place cakes on boards.

Dark chocolate ganache

Bring cream to a boil in medium saucepan, pour over chocolate in large bowl; stir until smooth. Cover bowl; refrigerate, about 30 minutes or until ganache is of a spreadable consistency.

Almond buttercake

150g butter, softened
½ teaspoon almond essence
⅔ cup (150g) caster sugar
2 eggs
⅓ cup (50g) self-raising flour
½ cup (75g) plain flour
½ cup (60g) ground almonds

Choux pastry

60g butter
¾ cup (180ml) water
¾ cup (105g) plain flour
3 eggs, beaten lightly

Vanilla custard

1¼ cups (310ml) milk
1 vanilla pod, split
4 egg yolks
½ cup (110g) caster sugar
¼ cup (40g) cornflour

Toffee

1 cup (220g) caster sugar
½ cup (125ml) water

1 Make choux pastry; make vanilla custard.
2 Preheat oven to moderate (180°C/160°C fan-assisted). Line 6-hole large or 12-hole standard muffin tray with paper cases.
3 Beat butter, essence, sugar and eggs in small bowl with electric mixer until light and fluffy.
4 Stir in sifted flours and ground almonds, in two batches. Divide mixture among cases; smooth surface.
5 Bake large cakes about 30 minutes, small cakes about 20 minutes. Turn cakes onto wire rack to cool.
6 Cut a 2cm deep hole in the centre of each cake, fill with custard; replace lid.
7 Spread tops of cakes with a little more custard. Top with a layer of puffs. Stack remaining puffs on cakes dipping each in a little custard.
8 Make toffee; drizzle over puffs.

Choux pastry

Preheat oven to hot (220°C/ 200°C fan-assisted). Grease oven trays, line with baking parchment. Combine butter with the water in medium saucepan; bring to a boil. Add flour; beat with wooden spoon over heat until mixture forms a smooth ball. Transfer mixture to small bowl; beat in egg with electric mixer in about six batches until mixture becomes glossy. Spoon mixture into piping bag fitted with 1cm plain tube. Pipe about 300 tiny dollops of pastry (about ¼ level teaspoon) 2cm apart, onto trays (see page 122); bake 7 minutes. Reduce oven to moderate (180°C/160°C fan-assisted); bake for further 5 minutes or until puffs are crisp. Repeat with remaining mixture.

Vanilla custard

Bring milk and vanilla pod to a boil in small saucepan; discard vanilla pod. Meanwhile, beat egg yolks, sugar and cornflour in small bowl with electric mixer until thick. With motor operating, gradually beat in warm milk. Return custard to same pan; stir over heat until mixture boils and thickens. Cover surface of custard with cling film; cool.

Toffee

Combine sugar with the water in small heavy-based saucepan. Stir over heat, without boiling, until sugar dissolves; bring to a boil. Reduce heat; simmer, uncovered, without stirring, until mixture is golden brown. Remove from heat; stand until bubbles subside before using.

toffee tumbles

apple custard tea cakes

Apple custard tea cakes

90g butter
½ teaspoon vanilla extract
½ cup (110g) caster sugar
2 eggs
¾ cup (110g) self-raising flour
¼ cup (30g) custard powder
2 tablespoons milk
1 large (200g) unpeeled apple,
   cored, sliced finely
30g butter, extra, melted
1 tablespoon caster sugar, extra
½ teaspoon ground cinnamon

Custard

1 tablespoon custard powder
1 tablespoon caster sugar
½ cup (125ml) milk
¼ teaspoon vanilla extract

1 Make custard.
2 Preheat oven to moderate (180°C/160°C fan-assisted). Line 6-hole large or 12-hole standard muffin tray with paper cases.
3 Beat butter, extract, sugar, eggs, flour, custard powder and milk in small bowl with electric mixer on low speed until ingredients are just combined. Increase speed to medium, beat until mixture is changed to a paler colour.
4 Divide half the mixture among cases. Top with custard, then remaining cake mixture; spread mixture to cover custard. Top with apple slices, pressing slightly into cake.
5 Bake large cakes about 40 minutes, small cakes about 30 minutes.
6 Brush hot cakes with extra butter, then sprinkle with combined extra sugar and cinnamon. Turn cakes onto wire rack. Serve warm or cold.

Custard

Blend custard powder and sugar with milk and extract in small saucepan; stir over heat until mixture boils and thickens. Remove from heat; cover surface with cling film; cool.

flower cakes

Banana sour cream cake

90g butter, softened
½ cup (110g) firmly packed
   brown sugar
2 eggs
½ cup (75g) self-raising flour
½ cup (75g) plain flour
½ teaspoon bicarbonate of soda
½ teaspoon mixed spice
⅔ cup (200g) mashed overripe
   banana
⅓ cup (80g) sour cream
2 tablespoons milk

Modelling fondant

2 teaspoons gelatine
1½ tablespoons water
2 teaspoons glucose syrup
1½ cups (240g) icing sugar
½ cup (80g) icing sugar, extra

Cream cheese frosting

30g butter, softened
80g cream cheese, softened
1½ cups (240g) icing sugar
blue food colouring

Decorations

½ cup (80g) icing sugar
400g white prepared fondant
   icing
pink and yellow food colouring
pink petal dust

1 Make modelling fondant. On a surface dusted with extra sifted icing sugar, roll modelling fondant to approximately 3mm thick. Cut out butterfly wings using butterfly cutter and shape butterfly bodies (see page 120); allow to dry.

2 Preheat oven to moderate (180°C/160°C fan-assisted). Line 6-hole large or 12-hole standard muffin tray with paper cases.

3 Beat butter, sugar and eggs in small bowl with electric mixer until light and fluffy.

4 Stir in sifted dry ingredients, then banana, cream and milk. Divide mixture among cases; smooth surface.

4 Bake large cakes about 35 minutes, small cakes about 25 minutes. Turn cakes onto wire rack to cool.

5 Make cream cheese frosting. Assemble butterflies (see pages 120 and 121).

6 On surface dusted with sifted icing sugar, knead prepared fondant icing until smooth. Using colouring, tint three-quarters of the fondant pink and one-quarter yellow. Roll out pink fondant to a thickness of 5mm; cut out petal shapes to suit the size of the cakes. Shape yellow fondant into balls; gently flatten until large enough to form centre of flowers.

7 Spread cakes with frosting. Decorate with petals and centres. Position a butterfly on each cake; dust wings with pink petal dust (see page 115).

Modelling fondant

Sprinkle gelatine over the water in cup; stand cup in small saucepan of simmering water, stirring until gelatine is dissolved, add glucose. Sift half the icing sugar into medium bowl; stir in gelatine mixture. Gradually stir in remaining sifted icing sugar, knead on surface dusted with extra sifted icing sugar until smooth. Wrap tightly in cling film to prevent drying out.

Cream cheese frosting

Beat butter and cheese in small bowl with electric mixer until light and fluffy; gradually beat in sfited icing sugar. Tint with colouring.

100g dark eating chocolate,
  melted
⅓ cup (110g) chocolate
  hazelnut spread
¼ cup (25g) ground hazelnuts
1 tablespoon finely crushed ice
  cream wafer or cone
12 hazelnuts, toasted
1 tablespoon ground hazelnuts,
  extra

1 Using small, clean paint brush, paint chocolate thickly inside 12 x 2.5cm foil cases. Place cases on tray; refrigerate about 5 minutes or until chocolate sets. Peel away cases (see pages 116 and 117).
2 Combine spread and ground hazelnuts in small bowl; spoon mixture into piping bag fitted with 1.5cm fluted tube.
3 Divide pieces of wafer and hazelnuts among cases. Pipe chocolate mixture into cases. Sprinkle with a little extra ground hazelnuts.

chocolate hazelnut cups

We used green, orange and yellow paper muffin cases to match the decorations of these lovely little cakes.

Poppy seed citrus cake

¼ cup (40g) poppy seeds
2 tablespoons milk
125g butter, softened
1 teaspoon finely grated lemon rind
1 teaspoon finely grated lime rind
⅔ cup (150g) caster sugar
2 eggs
1 cup (150g) self-raising flour
⅓ cup (50g) plain flour
⅓ cup (40g) ground almonds
¼ cup (60ml) orange juice

Decorations

½ cup (80g) icing sugar
450g white prepared fondant icing
green, orange and yellow food colouring
⅓ cup (110g) orange marmalade, warmed, sieved
2 tablespoons green sprinkles
2 tablespoons orange sprinkles
2 tablespoons yellow sprinkles

1 Preheat oven to moderate (180°C/160°C fan-assisted). Line 6-hole large or 12-hole standard muffin tray with paper cases.
2 Combine seeds and milk in small bowl; stand 20 minutes.
3 Beat butter, rinds, sugar and eggs in small bowl with electric mixer until light and fluffy.
4 Stir in sifted flours, ground almonds, juice and poppy seed mixture. Divide mixture among cases; smooth surface.
5 Bake large cakes about 30 minutes, small cakes about 20 minutes. Turn cakes onto wire rack to cool.
6 On surface dusted with sifted icing sugar, knead fondant icing until smooth. Reserve 100g of fondant; enclose in cling film. Divide remaining fondant into three equal portions; tint green, orange and yellow by kneading in colouring (see page 120). Wrap separately in cling film.

7 Roll each of the coloured portions to a thickness of 5mm. Cut out rounds large enough to cover tops of cakes. Brush tops of cakes with marmalade, position rounds on cakes.
8 Roll reserved fondant into very thin lengths, cut off small pieces to represent seeds. Position lengths on top of cakes, using a little water, to represent segments.
9 Fill segments with matching coloured sprinkles; position fondant seeds.

sweet violet cakes

Lemon cream cheese cake

90g butter, softened
90g cream cheese, softened
2 teaspoons finely grated
   lemon rind
⅔ cup (150g) caster sugar
2 eggs
⅓ cup (50g) self-raising flour
½ cup (75g) plain flour

Lemon cream cheese frosting

30g butter, softened
80g cream cheese, softened
1 teaspoon finely grated
   lemon rind
1½ cups (240g) icing sugar

Decorations

tea-lights
fresh violets

1 Preheat oven to moderate (180°C/160°C fan-assisted). Line 6-hole large or 12-hole standard muffin tray with paper cases.
2 Beat butter, cheese, rind, sugar and eggs in small bowl with electric mixer until light and fluffy.
3 Add sifted flours; beat on low speed until just combined. Divide mixture among cases; smooth surface.
4 Bake large cakes about 35 minutes, small cakes about 25 minutes. Turn cakes onto wire rack to cool.
5 Make lemon cream cheese frosting. Spread cakes with frosting; decorate with tea-lights and violets.

Lemon cream cheese frosting

Beat butter, cream cheese and rind in small bowl with electric mixer until light and fluffy; gradually beat in sifted icing sugar.

Cherry chocolate mud cake

425g can pitted cherries in syrup
165g butter, chopped coarsely
100g dark eating chocolate,
  chopped coarsely
1⅓ cups (295g) caster sugar
¼ cup (60ml) cherry brandy
1 cup (150g) plain flour
2 tablespoons self-raising flour
2 tablespoons cocoa powder
1 egg

Decorations

⅔ cup (160ml) whipping cream,
  whipped
2 teaspoons cherry brandy
100g dark eating chocolate

black forest cakes

1 Preheat oven to moderately low (170°C/150°C fan-assisted). Line 6-hole large or 12-hole standard muffin tray with paper cases.
2 Drain cherries; reserve syrup. Process ½ cup (110g) cherries with ½ cup (125ml) of the syrup until smooth. Halve remaining cherries; reserve for decorating cakes. Discard remaining syrup.
3 Combine butter, chocolate, sugar, brandy and cherry purée in small saucepan; stir over low heat until chocolate is melted. Transfer mixture to medium bowl; cool 15 minutes.
4 Whisk in sifted flours and cocoa, then egg. Divide mixture among cases; smooth surface.
5 Bake large cakes about 55 minutes, small cakes about 45 minutes. Turn cakes onto wire rack to cool.
6 Top cakes with remaining cherry halves and combined cream and cherry brandy. Using a vegetable peeler, make small chocolate curls (see page 116); sprinkle over cakes.

passionfruit curd cakes

Passionfruit buttercake

90g butter, softened
½ cup (110g) caster sugar
2 eggs
1 cup (150g) self-raising flour
¼ cup (60ml) passionfruit pulp

Passionfruit curd

2 eggs, beaten lightly
⅓ cup caster sugar
1 tablespoon lemon juice
¼ cup passionfruit pulp
60g butter, chopped coarsely

Decorations

85g packet passionfruit jelly
1 cup (250ml) boiling water
1 cup (80g) desiccated coconut
½ cup (125ml) whipping cream, whipped

1 Make passionfruit curd.
2 Preheat oven to moderate (180°C/160°C fan-assisted). Line 6-hole large or 12-hole standard muffin tray with paper cases.
3 Beat butter, sugar, eggs and flour in small bowl with electric mixer on low speed until ingredients are just combined. Increase speed to medium, beat until mixture is changed to a paler colour. Stir in passionfruit pulp.
4 Divide mixture among cases; smooth surface.
5 Bake large cakes about 25 minutes, small cakes about 20 minutes. Turn cakes onto wire rack to cool.
6 Dissolve jelly in the water. Refrigerate about 30 minutes or until set to the consistency of unbeaten egg white.
7 Remove cases from cakes. Roll cakes in jelly; leave cakes to stand in jelly for 15 minutes turning occasionally. Roll cakes in coconut; place on wire rack over tray. Refrigerate 30 minutes.
8 Cut cakes in half; fill with curd and cream.

Passionfruit curd

Combine ingredients in a small heatproof bowl, place over a small saucepan of simmering water; stir constantly until mixture thickens slightly and coats the back of a spoon. Remove from heat. Cover tightly; refrigerate curd until cold.

Orange almond cake

6 slices (120g) glacé orange
75g butter, softened
1 teaspoon finely grated
  orange rind
⅓ cup (75g) caster sugar
1 egg
2 tablespoons self-raising flour
¼ cup (35g) plain flour
¼ cup (30g) ground almonds

Decorations

15cm polystyrene craft ball
24 double-ended wooden
  toothpicks
2 sheets tissue paper
ribbon
fresh flowers
florist tape

1 Cut each orange slice into 20 tiny wedges.

2 Preheat oven to moderate (180°C/160°C fan-assisted). Line two 12-hole mini muffin pans with paper cases.

3 Beat butter, rind, sugar and egg in small bowl with electric mixer until light and fluffy.

4 Stir in sifted flours and ground almonds. Divide mixture among cases; smooth surface. Top each cake with five orange wedges.

5 Bake cakes about 15 minutes. Turn cakes onto wire rack to cool.

6 Using a serrated knife cut about quarter of the ball away, so the ball will sit flat. Using toothpicks, secure cakes to ball. Place bouquet on a small stand; wrap with paper and ribbon. Bind ends of fresh flowers with florist tape; position flowers between cakes.

orange bouquet

no-bake chocolate cakes

5 x 60g Mars bars
50g butter
3½ cups (120g) Rice Krispies
200g milk eating chocolate,
   melted

1 Line a 12-hole standard muffin tray with paper cases.
2 Chop four of the Mars bars coarsely; cut remaining bar into slices.
3 Place chopped bars in medium saucepan with butter; stir over low heat until smooth. Stir in Rice Krispies.
4 Press mixture into cases, spread with chocolate; top with sliced Mars bar. Refrigerate about 30 minutes or until set.

pineapple hibiscus cakes

Pineapple carrot cake

½ cup (125ml) vegetable oil
3 eggs, beaten lightly
1½ cups (225g) self-raising flour
¾ cup (165g) caster sugar
½ teaspoon ground cinnamon
2 cups (440g) firmly packed
   coarsely grated carrot
¾ cup (160g) drained crushed
   pineapple

Pineapple flowers

1 tablespoon caster sugar
1 tablespoon water
12 wafer thin slices fresh
   pineapple

Lemon cream cheese frosting

30g butter, softened
80g cream cheese, softened
1 teaspoon finely grated
   lemon rind
1½ cups (240g) icing sugar

1 Make pineapple flowers.
2 Preheat oven to moderate
(180°C/160°C fan-assisted).
Line a 6-hole large or 12-hole
standard muffin tray with
paper cases.
3 Combine oil, eggs, flour, sugar
and cinnamon in medium bowl;
stir until combined. Stir in carrot
and pineapple.
4 Divide mixture among cases.
5 Bake large cakes about
40 minutes, small cakes about
30 minutes. Turn cakes onto
wire rack to cool.
6 Make lemon cream cheese
frosting; spread on top of cakes.
Decorate with pineapple flowers.

Pineapple flowers

Preheat oven to very low
(120°C/100°C fan-assisted).
Stir sugar and the water together
in a small saucepan over low
heat until sugar has dissolved;
boil 1 minute. Brush both
sides of pineapple slices with
sugar syrup. Place slices in a
single layer on wire racks over
oven trays (see page 125). Dry
pineapple in oven for about
1 hour. Immediately remove
slices from rack; carefully shape
into flowers. Dry over an egg
carton (see page 125).

Lemon cream cheese frosting

Beat butter, cream cheese and
rind in small bowl with electric
mixer until light and fluffy;
gradually beat in sifted icing sugar.

chocolate ginger rose buds

Chocolate ginger mud cake

165g butter, chopped coarsely
100g dark eating chocolate,
    chopped coarsely
1⅓ cups (295g) caster sugar
⅔ cup (160ml) green ginger wine
¼ cup (60ml) water
1 cup (150g) plain flour
2 tablespoons self-raising flour
2 tablespoons cocoa powder
1 egg
⅓ cup (75g) finely chopped
    glacé ginger

Chocolate decorations

100g dark eating chocolate,
    melted
100g milk eating chocolate,
    melted
fresh rose leaves, washed

Dark chocolate ganache

½ cup (125ml) whipping cream
200g dark eating chocolate,
    chopped coarsely

1 Make chocolate decorations
– rose buds, stems and leaves.
2 Preheat oven to moderately
low (170°C/150°C fan-assisted).
Line 6-hole large or 12-hole
standard muffin tray with
paper cases.
3 Combine butter, chocolate,
sugar, ginger wine and the water
in small saucepan; stir over low
heat until smooth. Transfer to
medium bowl; cool 15 minutes.
4 Whisk in sifted flours and
cocoa, then egg. Stir in ginger.
Divide mixture among cases.
5 Bake large cakes about 1 hour,
small cakes about 50 minutes.
Turn cakes onto wire rack to cool.
6 Make dark chocolate ganache.
7 Pour ganache over cakes; set
at room temperature.
8 Decorate cakes with chocolate
rose buds, stems and leaves.

Chocolate decorations

For rose buds, spread dark
chocolate onto a cold surface;
when set, pull a melon baller over
chocolate to make rose buds
(see page 116). For stems, spoon
half the milk chocolate into paper
piping bag (see page 117); pipe
stems onto a baking parchment-
lined tray (see page 117); leave
to set. Gently lift stems off paper.
For leaves, using a small, clean
paint brush, paint remaining milk
chocolate thickly on one side of
each leaf (see page 116), place on
baking parchment-lined tray; leave
to set. Carefully peel away and
discard leaves (see page 117).

Dark chocolate ganache

Bring cream to a boil in small
saucepan; pour over chocolate
in small bowl; stir until smooth.
Stand at room temperature
until ganache is a thick pouring
consistency.

easter egg baskets

Light fruit cake

Light fruit cake

125g butter, softened
½ teaspoon almond essence
⅔ cup (150g) caster sugar
2 eggs
⅔ cup (140g) red and green
  glacé cherries, quartered
⅓ cup (55g) sultanas
½ cup (70g) slivered almonds
⅔ cup (100g) plain flour
⅓ cup (50g) self-raising flour
¼ cup (60ml) milk

Royal icing

3 cups (480g) icing sugar
2 egg whites
1 teaspoon lemon juice
brown food colouring

Decorations

300g sugared almonds or
  mini chocolate eggs

1 Preheat oven to moderately low (170°C/150°C fan-assisted). Line 6-hole large or 12-hole standard muffin tray with paper cases.
2 Beat butter, essence, sugar and eggs in small bowl with electric mixer until light and fluffy.
3 Add fruit and nuts; mix well. Stir in sifted flours and milk. Divide mixture among cases; smooth surface.
4 Bake large cakes about 45 minutes, small cakes about 40 minutes. Turn cakes onto wire rack to cool.
5 Make royal icing.
6 Remove cases from cakes. Pipe basket weave around cakes (see page 123); leave to dry for 3 hours or overnight.
7 Fill baskets with sugared almonds or chocolate eggs.

Royal icing

Sift icing sugar through very fine sieve. Lightly beat egg whites in small bowl with electric mixer; beat in icing sugar, a tablespoon at a time. When icing reaches firm peaks, use wooden spoon to beat in juice and colouring; cover tightly with cling film.

spicy christmas cakes

Make these festive cupcakes
for Christmas; serve warm with
brandy butter, whipped cream
or custard.

Buttermilk spice cake

½ cup (110g) firmly packed
    brown sugar
½ cup (75g) plain flour
½ cup (75g) self-raising flour
¼ teaspoon bicarbonate of soda
1 teaspoon ground ginger
½ teaspoon ground cinnamon
¼ teaspoon ground nutmeg
90g butter, softened
1 egg
¼ cup (60ml) buttermilk
2 tablespoons golden syrup

Christmas decorations

½ cup (80g) icing sugar
100g white prepared fondant
    icing
5cm lengths of covered
    24 gauge wire

Filling

½ cup (180g) mincemeat
1 tablespoon icing sugar

1 Make Christmas decorations.
2 Preheat oven to moderate
(180°C/160°C fan-assisted). Line
6-hole large or 12-hole standard
muffin tray with paper cases.
3 Sift dry ingredients into small
bowl, add remaining ingredients;
beat with electric mixer on low
speed until ingredients are
combined. Increase speed to
medium, beat until mixture is
smooth and changed to a paler
colour. Divide mixture among
cases; smooth surface.
4 Bake large cakes about
35 minutes, small cakes about
25 minutes. Turn cakes onto
wire rack to cool for 5 minutes.
5 Make filling. Cut a 2cm deep
hole in the centre of each warm
cake; discard cake rounds. Fill
centres with filling mixture. Top
with wired fondant shapes; dust
with a little sifted icing sugar.

Christmas decorations

On surface dusted with sifted
icing sugar, knead fondant
icing until smooth. Roll out to
1cm thickness. Cut out fondant
shapes using Christmas cutters
(see page 115). Insert a length
of damp wire into each shape.
Dry overnight on baking
parchment-lined tray.

Filling

Warm mincemeat in small
saucepan over low heat; stir in
icing sugar. Or, heat mincemeat
in a microwave oven for about
30 seconds on HIGH (100%); stir
in icing sugar.

christmas tree cakes

Tropical fruit cake

125g butter, softened
1 teaspoon coconut essence
⅔ cup (150g) caster sugar
2 eggs
1 cup (180g) finely chopped
   dried tropical fruit salad
½ cup (75g) macadamia nuts,
   chopped coarsely
⅔ cup (100g) plain flour
⅓ cup (50g) self-raising flour
⅓ cup (25g) desiccated coconut
¼ cup (60ml) milk

Coconut ice frosting

2 egg whites
1 teaspoon coconut essence
1½ cups (240g) icing sugar
1 cup (90g) desiccated coconut

Decorations

10 star fruit, approximately
green edible glitter

1 Preheat oven to moderately
low (170°C/150°C fan-assisted).
Line 6-hole large or 12-hole
standard muffin tray with
paper cases.
2 Beat butter, essence, sugar
and eggs in small bowl with
electric mixer until light and fluffy.
3 Stir in dried fruit and nuts, then
sifted flours, coconut and milk.
Divide mixture among cases;
smooth surface.
4 Bake large cakes about
45 minutes, small cakes about
35 minutes. Turn cakes onto
wire racks to cool.
5 Make coconut ice frosting;
top cakes with frosting.
6 Cut star fruit into 5mm slices.
Arrange slices to make Christmas
tree shapes of varying heights
and sizes depending on size
of cakes used. Use toothpicks
or trimmed bamboo skewers
to hold star fruit in position.
Sprinkle with glitter.

Coconut ice frosting

Beat egg whites and essence
in small bowl with electric mixer
until foamy. Beat in sifted icing
sugar in about four batches; stir
in coconut.

christmas snowflakes

Rich fruit cake

90g butter, softened
½ cup (110g) firmly packed
   brown sugar
2 eggs
1 tablespoon orange marmalade
500g (2¾ cups) mixed dried fruit,
   chopped finely
⅔ cup (100g) plain flour
2 tablespoons self-raising flour
1 teaspoon mixed spice
2 tablespoons sweet sherry
2 tablespoons sweet sherry, extra

Decorations

½ cup (80g) icing sugar
300g white prepared fondant
   icing
½ teaspoon edible silver lustre
½ teaspoon vodka
silver cachous
⅓ cup (110g) apricot jam,
   warmed, sieved

1 Preheat oven to low (150°C/130°C fan-assisted). Line 6-hole large muffin or 12-hole standard tray with paper cases.

2 Beat butter, sugar and eggs in small bowl with electric mixer until just combined.

3 Stir in marmalade and fruit; mix well.

4 Sift flours and spice over mixture; add sherry, mix well. Divide mixture among cases; smooth surface.

5 Bake large cakes about 1 hour, small cakes about 50 minutes. Remove cakes from oven; brush tops with extra sherry. Cover tray tightly with foil; cool cakes in tray.

6 On surface dusted with sifted icing sugar, knead fondant icing until smooth; roll out to a thickness of 5mm. Using a fluted cutter, cut out rounds large enough to almost cover tops of cakes.

7 Using a cardboard snowflake template (see page 115), gently press an imprint into the centre of each fondant round (see page 125).

8 Brush cakes with jam; top with fondant rounds. Blend lustre with vodka, paint onto snowflakes; push silver cachous gently into rounds.

jewelettes

Festive jewel cake

2 rings (55g) glacé pineapple
3 whole (85g) glacé apricots
1 cup (140g) stoneless dried
  dates
⅔ cup (140g) red and green
  glacé cherries
½ cup (80g) whole blanched
  almonds
1 cup (160g) brazil nuts
2 eggs
⅓ cup (75g) firmly packed
  brown sugar
1 tablespoon dark rum
60g butter, softened
¼ cup (35g) plain flour
2 tablespoons self-raising flour

Topping

3 rings (80g) glacé pineapple
½ cup (100g) red and green
  glacé cherries, halved
½ cup (80g) brazil nuts
½ cup (80g) whole blanched
  almonds
⅓ cup (110g) apricot jam,
  warmed, sieved

1 Preheat oven to low (150°C/
130°C fan-assisted). Line 6-hole
large or 12-hole standard muffin
tray with paper cases.
2 Coarsely chop pineapple and
apricots, halve cherries and
nuts for large cakes. Chop
fruit and nuts slightly smaller
for small cakes.
3 Combine fruit and nuts in
medium bowl.
4 Beat eggs in small bowl with
electric mixer until thick and
creamy; add sugar, rum and
butter, beat until just combined.
5 Stir egg mixture into fruit
mixture with sifted flours. Divide
mixture among cases; press
firmly into cases.
6 Make topping; divide evenly
over cakes.
7 Bake large cakes about
1¼ hours, small cakes about
1 hour; cover cakes loosely with
foil halfway through baking time.
Cool cakes in tray.
8 Remove cakes from tray; brush
tops with jam.

Topping

Coarsely chop pineapple;
combine with remaining fruit
and nuts for large cakes. Chop
fruit and nuts slightly smaller for
small cakes. Combine fruit and
nuts in small bowl; mix well.

equipment

1. Piping bags
Available from cake decorating shops, chefs' supply shops and cookware shops, these are usually made from a waterproof fabric. Bags can also be made from baking or greaseproof paper; ideal for small amounts of icing (see page 117).

2. Rolling pins, brushes and metal spatulas
Mini rolling pins are available from cake decorating shops; fine artists' brushes from stationers, and metal spatulas from cookware shops.

3. Florist tape and wire
These are used to hold flowers and fondant shapes in position. Always cover wire or flower stems with florist tape if they are to be inserted into icing or cake.

4. Cutters
Come in all shapes and sizes; available from cake decorating or chefs' suppliers; these are usually made from metal or plastic.

5. Muffin trays
Each recipe specifies the required muffin tray size – large, medium and small:
6-hole large (¾ cup/180ml)
12-hole standard (⅓ cup/80ml)
12-hole mini (1 tablespoon/20ml)

6. Paper and foil cases
Each recipe specifies the required paper case size, this denotes the tray size. Measured across the base: large muffin 6.5cm, freeform 6cm, standard muffin 5cm, mini muffin 3cm, foil cases 2.5cm. Paper cases are available from cake decorating shops, chefs' supply shops, supermarkets and cookware shops.

7. Lustre and edible glitter
Lustre is a powder available from cake decorating suppliers and craft shops in metallic shades, and is applied with a paintbrush. It is considered 'edible' in Europe and classified non-toxic for decoration only in Australia and the United States. Edible glitter is a non-metallic decoration for cakes.

8. Templates, lace and stamps
Templates and rubber stamps can be bought from cake decorating shops, craft shops and some stationers.

9. Colourings
Many types are available from cake decorating suppliers, craft shops and some supermarkets; all are concentrated. Use a minute amount of any type of colouring first to determine its strength. They are also available in liquid, gel, powder and paste forms. Powdered are edible and are used when primary colours or black are needed. Concentrated pastes are a little more expensive but are the easiest to use; are suitable for both pastel and stronger colours.

10. Flower making tools
A ball tool is used to shape petals and flowers; a frilling tool is used to shape lily petals; stamens are used for flower centres. These can all be bought from specialist cake decorating suppliers.

11. Icing tubes
Are made from metal or plastic, and can be bought from cake decorating suppliers, some craft shops, supermarkets and cookware shops.

Melting chocolate
Place coarsely chopped chocolate in small heatproof bowl, over small saucepan of simmering water; stir occasionally, until chocolate is melted. It is important that water not be allowed to come in contact with the chocolate, if it does it will sieze. You can melt chocolate in a microwave oven; melt on MEDIUM (55%) about 1 minute, stirring twice during melting.

Making small chocolate curls
Using a sharp vegetable peeler, scrape along the side of a long piece of room-temperature eating-quality chocolate. Clean the peeler often so that the chocolate doesn't clog the surface of the blade.

Making chocolate curls using melon baller
Spread melted chocolate evenly and thinly onto a piece of marble, laminated board or flat oven tray; stand at room temperature until just set but not hard. Pull a melon baller over the surface of chocolate to make curls. We used these as rose buds (see page 103).

Painting foil cases & leaves with chocolate
Use a fine clean, dry paintbrush. Paint melted chocolate thickly inside each foil case or onto one side of a clean freshly-picked leaf; leave to set at room temperature.

Finishing chocolate foil cases & leaves

Carefully peel back case or leaf from chocolate. These can be made ahead and stored in an airtight container at room temperature until required. If the weather is hot, keep them in the refrigerator.

Colouring white chocolate

Using a skewer, add a few drops of colouring (the amount depends on the intensity of the colouring) into melted white chocolate and stir with a clean dry spoon, until colour is even. Too much colouring will cause chocolate to seize, that is, clump and turn an unappealing colour.

Making a piping bag

Cut a 30cm square of baking parchment or greaseproof paper in half diagonally; hold apex of one triangle towards you. Twist first one point, then the other, into a cone shape. Bring three points together; secure the three points with a staple; repeat with other triangle. Sticky tape will hold a greaseproof bag together, but not one made from baking parchment.

Piping chocolate

Place melted chocolate into paper piping bag. Snip end from bag. Cover an oven tray with baking parchment, pipe desired shapes; leave to set at room temperature. Gently lift chocolate shapes from paper.

Making sugar syrup

Always place sugar and water in recommended size heavy-based saucepan. To prevent crystallisation or graininess, the sugar must be completely dissolved before the mixture boils. Stir constantly over medium to high heat to dissolve sugar. If sugar grains stick to the side of the pan, use a clean pastry brush dipped in water to brush down the sides of the pan.

Boiling sugar syrup

After sugar syrup comes to a boil, do not stir, and do not scrape pan or stir the syrup during cooking. Boil the syrup for about 5 minutes or until thick. Remove pan from heat; allow bubbles to subside before using. This stage can be measured accurately by buying a sugar thermometer. The temperature should be 118°C. This stage is perfect for fluffy frosting.

Boiling sugar syrup to hard crack

Bring sugar syrup to a boil, reduce heat; simmer uncovered, without stirring for about 10 minutes or until mixture is golden. Remove from heat; stand until bubbles subside before using. If using a sugar thermometer, mixture should be between 138°C and 154°C depending on the colour required. The longer the toffee boils and colours the harder it will set.

Sugar thermometer

Thermometer should be stainless steel and have a clip to attach to the pan. Once sugar is dissolved, place thermometer in small saucepan of cold water (mercury must be covered). Bring the water to a boil, check thermometer for accuracy at boiling point. When sugar syrup comes to a boil, place thermometer in syrup (mercury must be covered). Boil to the required temperature. Return thermometer to pan of boiling water, remove from heat, allow thermometer to cool in the water.

Checking toffee for hard crack

To test toffee for hard crack use a clean dry spoon and carefully drizzle some toffee into cold water. If it has reached hard crack it should set immediately. Always remove the pan from the heat and allow the bubbles to subside before testing.

Testing toffee

Remove set toffee from cold water and snap between fingers. It should be brittle and snap easily.

Making toffee shards

When toffee reaches a golden colour, remove pan from heat, allow bubbles to subside; drizzle toffee from the back of a wooden spoon, onto a baking parchment-lined oven tray. Allow toffee to set at room temperature. Remove shards from paper using a spatula. Immediately position on cake.

Shaping toffee over rolling pin

When toffee reaches a golden colour, remove pan from heat, allow bubbles to subside. Drizzle toffee from wooden spoon onto a rolling pin, covered with baking parchment. Allow toffee to set at room temperature. Slide baking parchment off rolling pin to remove toffee shapes. Immediately position on cake.

Colouring prepared fondant icing
After kneading fondant icing until smooth, use a skewer to colour fondant; kneading colouring into fondant until desired colour is achieved. The amount of colouring needed will depend on the intensity of the colouring used.

Covering cakes with prepared almond paste or fondant icing
Brush cakes lightly and evenly with jam. Roll almond paste or fondant icing to desired thickness; lift onto cake with hands or rolling pin. Smooth surface with hands dusted with icing sugar, ease paste or fondant around side and base of cake; trim excess with sharp knife.

Shaping flowers from modelling fondant
Cut out flowers using cutter of choice, place flower on clean folded tea towel. Using ball tool, gently shape flower; leave to dry.

Making butterfy from modelling fondant
Roll out fondant to 2mm thick. Cut out wings, place damp wire into each wing; dry flat. Make body of butterfly by moulding a piece of fondant; attach wire to body.

Shaping butterfly
Bring wires, with wings attached, together. Use florist tape to secure wires and shape butterfly.

Making lily petals from modelling fondant
Knead fondant; roll to a thickness of 2mm. Using the lily petal cutter, cut out 6 petals for each flower. Frill along each edge, using thicker edge of frilling tool. Gently score two lines on each petal.

Drying lily petals
Dry individual petals in round-based bun trays or soup spoons. Bend the wire at a 90° angle from the petal.

Assembling lily
Wet one end of single wire lengths, insert into end of each petal; dry on baking parchment-lined tray. For flower centre (pistle), roll tiny balls of fondant icing. Wet one end of single wire length, insert into balls; pinch balls several times with tweezers. To assemble lily, attach five stamens to pistle with florist tape. Attach one to two petals at a time, around pistle, using florist tape.

Piping choux pastry

Spoon choux pastry into piping bag fitted with a 1cm plain tube. Hold piping bag vertical to baking parchment-lined oven tray; quickly pivot wrist, piping tiny dollops (equal to ¼ teaspoon) of choux pastry 2cm apart, onto tray.

Piping meringue

Spoon meringue into piping bag fitted with a 1cm plain tube. Hold piping bag vertical to the cake, piping a spiral from the outside to the centre of the cake.

Piping lines with royal icing

Spoon icing into piping bag fitted with a small plain tube. Gently touch surface with tip of tube, lightly squeezing piping bag. As icing comes out, lift tube up from surface, squeezing to desired length. Stop squeezing bag, placing icing down onto surface. Even pressure is paramount – too much will give uneven thickness, too little pressure and the line will break.

Piping cornelli pattern with royal icing

Spoon icing into piping bag fitted with a small plain tube. Hold tube tip close to cake surface so that icing attaches without tube scraping cake or flattening the icing line. Pipe a continuous, meandering line of icing; move tip up, around and down to produce a lacy effect – don't let lines touch or cross.

Piping basket weave with royal icing

Using a basket weave tube, pipe a long vertical line from the top of the cake to the bottom, followed by short horizontal lines across the long vertical line. The horizontal lines should be a tube-width apart.

Pipe the next long vertical line at the end of the previous short horizontal lines.

Pipe short horizontal lines into the gaps, between the two vertical lines.

Repeat previous steps, continuing the basket weave design until the design meets with the starting point.

Shaping cakes
Using a serrated knife carefully shave edges of cake away.

Sugar-frosting fruit
Using a small clean paint brush, lightly and sparingly brush fruit individually with egg white; dip wet fruit in sugar. Place frosted fruit on baking parchment-lined tray. Leave about 1 hour or until sugar is dry.

Dusting-on designs
The best results are achieved by using several doilies still joined together, pieces of plastic backed lace tablecloths or thick fabric lace, as they are easier to lift away from the cake once dusted with icing sugar.

Feather and fan
Place chocolate topping into paper piping bag. Starting in the centre of the cream topped cake, pipe a spiral. Using a skewer, gently drag through the spiral design, from the cake centre to the edge of the paper case.

Drying pears and pineapple

Fruit needs to be sliced thinly and evenly – a mandoline or V-slicer is ideal, alternatively use a very sharp knife. Using a clean pastry brush, brush both sides of sliced fruit with sugar syrup. Place fruit on wire rack over an oven tray. Bake for specified time.

Shaping dried pears and pineapple

Dried fruit slices must be lifted from wire rack immediately after baking to prevent sticking. For pear slices, shape by pinching narrow end; dry on wire rack. For pineapple slices, pinch centre of each slice; dry over egg carton.

Colouring sugar

Use granulated or caster sugar, depending on the texture you prefer. Place required amount of sugar in a plastic bag, add a tiny amount of colouring; work colouring through sugar by 'massaging' plastic bag. Sugar will keep in a jar at room temperature indefinitely.

Marking fondant

Roll fondant icing to desired thickness; place textured templates onto fondant, pressing gently to leave an imprint. Lift template away from fondant icing. Or, gently press cardboard stencil into fondant, leaving imprint. Paint imprint with colouring or fill with coloured sugar or sprinkles. Or, using a small, clean brush, paint design on stamp with coloured paste; gently press stamp onto fondant, to leave a coloured imprint.

glossary

after dinner mints mint squares coated in dark chocolate.

almonds
blanched brown skins removed.
flaked paper-thin slices.
ground also called almond meal.
slivered small lengthways-cut pieces.

bicarbonate of soda also known as baking soda.

brandy snap is a crisp wafer thin sweet biscuit.

butter use salted or unsalted ('sweet') butter; 125g is equal to 1 stick of butter.

buttermilk sold in the refrigerated dairy compartments in supermarkets. It is the liquid left after cream is separated from milk.

cachous small, round cake-decorating sweets available in silver, gold and various colours.

chocolate
dark we used premium-quality dark eating chocolate, not compound.
milk primarily for eating.
topping also called chocolate sauce.
white eating chocolate.

chocolate hazelnut spread also known as Nutella.

cocoa powder also known as cocoa; dried, unsweetened, roasted ground cocoa beans.

coconut
desiccated unsweetened and concentrated, dried finely shredded.
flaked dried flaked coconut flesh.
liqueur we used Malibu.
shredded thin strips of dried coconut flesh.

coffee-flavoured liqueur we used either Tia Maria or Kahlua.

cream, whipping a cream containing thickener with a minimum fat content of 35%.

cream cheese commonly known as Philadelphia or Philly, a soft cow-milk cheese with fat content of at least 33%.

coloured sprinkles also known as Dollar 5's.

custard powder instant mixture used to make pouring custard; similar to North American instant pudding mixes.

dried mixed berries lightly crunchy dehydrated form of strawberries, blueberries, cherries. They can be eaten as is or used as an ingredient in cooking.

dried fruit salad commonly made with tropical fruit like paw paw, pineapple and mango.

dulce de leche a sweet sauce made from condensed milk that has been boiled to a caramel.

eggs some recipes in this book call for raw or barely cooked eggs; these should be avoided by vulnerable people such as pregnant and nursing mothers, invalids, the elderly, babies and young children.

essence a synthetically produced substance used sparingly to impart flavour to foods.

Ferrero Raffaello is a crispy, creamy almond and coconut bite-sized sweet.

flour
cornflour also known as cornstarch.
plain an all-purpose flour, made from wheat.
self-raising plain (all purpose) flour sifted with baking powder in the proportion of 1 cup flour to 2 teaspoons baking powder.

gelatine (gelatin) we used powdered gelatine as a setting agent.

ginger wine made with a grape base to which ginger, spices, herbs and fruits have been added.

glacé fruits fruits that have been cooked in heavy syrup.

glucose syrup also known as liquid glucose; a sugary syrup made from starches such as wheat and corn.

golden syrup a by-product of refined sugarcane.

ground hazelnuts also called ground hazelnut meal.

jam also called preserve or conserve.

maple-flavoured syrup made from sugar cane rather than maple-tree sap; used in cooking or as a topping but cannot be considered an exact substitute for pure maple syrup.

marmalade is a jam or conserve made with shredded citrus rind.

marsala a sweet fortified wine originally from Sicily.

mascarpone a fresh, thick, triple-cream cheese with a delicately sweet, slightly sour taste.

milk we used full-cream homogenised milk.

mincemeat also called fruit mince; a sweet mixture of dried fruits, sugar, suet, nuts and flavourings.

mixed dried fruit also known as dried fruit; commonly a combination of sultanas, raisins, currants, mixed peel and cherries.

mixed spice a blend of ground spices usually consisting of cinnamon, allspice and nutmeg.

plain sweet biscuits un-iced plain biscuits or cookies used to make crumbs.

poppy seeds possessing a nutty, slightly sweet flavour and a dark blue-grey colour, come from capsules inside an opium plant indigenous to the Mediterranean.

prepared fondant icing also known as soft icing and ready-to-roll.

Rice Krispies also known as Rice Bubbles, are made of rice and are an example of a puffed grain cereal.

rind also known as zest.

rose petals, dried slightly chewy, dehydrated form of this popular flower. They can be used to flavour sweet and savoury dishes.
rosewater extract made from crushed rose petals, called gulab in India; used for its aromatic quality in many sweetmeats and desserts.
sour cream thick, commercially-cultured with a minimum fat content of 35%.
star fruit also known as carambola, five-corner fruit or Chinese star fruit.
sugar
brown a soft, fine granulated sugar containing molasses to give its characteristic colour.
caster also known as superfine or finely granulated table sugar.
granulated table sugar, coarser than caster sugar.
icing also called confectioners' or powdered sugar; crushed granulated sugar with added cornflour (about 3%).
vanilla is granulated or caster sugar flavoured with a vanilla pod. Can be stored indefinitely.
sultanas also called golden raisins.
vanilla
extract distilled from the seeds of the vanilla pod.
pod dried long, thin pod from a tropical golden orchid grown in Central and South America and Tahiti. Tiny black seeds inside the bean are used to impart a vanilla flavour in baking and desserts.
vegetable oil any of a number of oils sourced from plants rather than animal fats.
vodka clear, colourless, flavourless spirit that evaporates as it dries.

conversion chart

Measures

The cup and spoon measurements used in this book are metric: one measuring cup holds approximately 250ml; one metric tablespoon holds 20ml; one metric teaspoon holds 5ml.

All cup and spoon measurements are level. The most accurate way of measuring dry ingredients is to weigh them. When measuring liquids, use a clear glass or plastic jug with the metric markings.

We use large eggs with an average weight of 60g. This book contains recipes for dishes made with raw or lightly cooked eggs. These should be avoided by vulnerable people such as pregnant and nursing mothers, invalids, the elderly, babies and young children.

dry measures

METRIC	IMPERIAL
15g	½oz
30g	1oz
60g	2oz
90g	3oz
125g	4oz (¼lb)
155g	5oz
185g	6oz
220g	7oz
250g	8oz (½lb)
280g	9oz
315g	10oz
345g	11oz
375g	12oz (¾lb)
410g	13oz
440g	14oz
470g	15oz
500g	16oz (1lb)
750g	24oz (1½lb)
1kg	32oz (2lb)

liquid measures

METRIC	IMPERIAL
30ml	1 fluid oz
60ml	2 fluid oz
100ml	3 fluid oz
125ml	4 fluid oz
150ml	5 fluid oz (¼ pint/1 gill)
190ml	6 fluid oz
250ml	8 fluid oz
300ml	10 fluid oz (½ pint)
500ml	16 fluid oz
600ml	20 fluid oz (1 pint)
1000ml (1 litre)	1¾ pints

Length measures

3mm	⅛in
6mm	¼in
1cm	½in
2cm	¾in
2.5cm	1in
5cm	2in
6cm	2½in
8cm	3in
10cm	4in
13cm	5in
15cm	6in
18cm	7in
20cm	8in
23cm	9in
25cm	10in
28cm	11in
30cm	12in (1ft)

Oven temperatures

These oven temperatures are only a guide for conventional ovens. For fan-assisted ovens, check the manufacturer's manual.

	°C (CELSIUS)	°F (FAHRENHEIT)	GAS MARK
Very low	120	250	½
Low	150	275-300	1-2
Moderately low	170	325	3
Moderate	180	350-375	4-5
Moderately hot	200	400	6
Hot	220	425-450	7-8
Very hot	240	475	9